Shadow Lessons

Shadow Lessons

The Unexpected Journey of an Inner City Art Teacher

Daniel Bonnell

RESOURCE *Publications* • Eugene, Oregon

SHADOW LESSONS
The Unexpected Journey of an Inner City Art Teacher

Copyright © 2012 Daniel Bonnell. All rights reserved. Except for brief quotations in critical publications or reviews, no part of this book may be reproduced in any manner without prior written permission from the publisher. Write: Permissions, Wipf and Stock Publishers, 199 W. 8th Ave., Suite 3, Eugene, OR 97401.

Resource Publications
An Imprint of Wipf and Stock Publishers
199 W. 8th Ave., Suite 3
Eugene, OR 97401

www.wipfandstock.com

ISBN 13: 978-1-62032-543-8

Manufactured in the U.S.A.

To the love of my life, my wife Vicki.

Contents

Acknowledgements		ix
One	Matthew	1
Two	St. Paul's Cathedral	4
Three	Beginnings	8
Four	Diving in Shallow Water	13
Five	Corona Landscapes	15
Six	Surreal Fear	18
Seven	Four Point Perspective of Four Students	22
Eight	Rhythm	28
Nine	Special Needs Saints	31
Ten	Pastor Blade	34
Eleven	The Invisible	37
Twelve	The Hidden Masterpiece	43
Thirteen	Castles in the Sky	45
Fourteen	The Question	47
Fifteen	The Kitten	50
Sixteen	The Boss	55
Seventeen	The Scream	60
Eighteen	The Fight	64

Nineteen	Sally	67
Twenty	Illusions	70
Twenty One	Stormie	74
Twenty Two	Look Around	77
Twenty Three	Soul Food	80
Twenty Four	Being Thankful	82
Twenty Five	The Divine Proportion	85
Twenty Six	Dan the Pastry Man	88
Twenty Seven	Being Present	90
Twenty Eight	Herbie	93
Afterword		97
Endnotes		99

Acknowledgements

I WISH TO THANK Paul-Gordon Chandler and his wonderful wife Lynne, both angels incognito, for being my greatest patrons for over 20 years. Together you take the form of a Theo to this Vincent.

Chapter One

Matthew

Between our birth and death we may touch understanding, as a moth brushes a window with its wings.
—Christopher Fry

FROM DOWN THE HALL the screams flooded into Matthew's room. A flash flood of fear filled his room. It was after 2 am in the projects of Savannah. If the loud screaming had not wakened him surely his pool of sweltering sweat would have. His mother's enraged boyfriend, another pretender of a man in a boy's body chose to look on his mother as just another whore, as he was chopping into her soul with a vulgar tongue like some kind of manic butcher. This was nothing new to Matthew. Though just a tender eight years old, he'd already been couched in the abrasive culture around him to a vocabulary of profanity twice his age, and violence most people only see on the news in war-torn countries.

Curled up in bed and gripping his tattered pillow for comfort, he stoically gazed out his window trying to escape the moment. It was as if the full moon had cast light into his room just to comfort him for the moment. Just another hot Savannah night, he kept reassuring himself, trying to excuse the crudeness penetrating his walls and ears.

His moon view allowed him to see the long row of shotgun houses that had been built and rebuilt over the past 130 years by slaves, their children, and their children's children. They are called shotgun houses because if you pulled the trigger on a shotgun from the front door, the pellets would go right out the back door. The railroad-car-designed homes were built side by side, so close to one another that you could reach out your window and almost touch the house next door. The homes fostered a different kind of community that few white folks had ever known. Add barbed wire and you'd have a concentration camp.

Matthew's moonbeam escape lasted all of about a minute. He was shocked out of his trance by a crescendo of "Fuck!" and every form of it—angrily shouted in his mother's room over, and over, and over. He pressed his hands against his ears, squeezed his eyes tightly shut, and clenched his teeth hard, trying to mentally wash it all away as it poured into his mildew smelling room. Then . . . "BAM!" His eyes burst open. His jaw dropped. Matthew, shaking and terrified, dug his hands hard into his pillow and curled up into a ball pretending to be invisible under his single bed sheet. Fearfully he listened to the heavy stomping of footsteps racing down the hall, the front door slamming, and the penetrating noise of tires screaming off into the night. They were the final sounds of the longest night of his young life, the sounds that brought his world and his mother to a complete silence. How he so badly wanted a father to save the day and come to the rescue. But his father, like most of the fathers of the kids he knew, was just another snake who would love in pretence, lay his eggs, and run off with another woman before Matthew was even born.

With his weakened legs trembling and heart vociferously pounding, Matthew inched out of bed, slowly opened his creaking door, and poked his head out. A thin stream of smoke and the smell of gunpowder were floating through the air of the long, narrow hallway lit by a lone, dim light bulb. Matthew forced his heavy feet to move before him as he warily followed the smoke to his mother's room. In a shadowed filled room that deflected light from a glaring streetlamp into a curtain-less box, he came upon her lying perfectly still on her back. Her still, solid black profile was projected on the wall.

"Mama?" he asked softly.

A decade later, it was a night from which Matthew still had not awoken as he sat at his desk in the same fearful silence, staring out the window in my first period art class, just like he stared at that full moon and his mother's shadowed profile. There were 35 students in this first class of my first week of my first year of teaching. I would eventually discover that behind each of my students' curtain of a young life there laid a drama such as Matthew's of which I had no conception. It would take months, even years, for me to discover my blindness as I sat in the front row of this culturally slave beaten theatre called Beach High School.

Chapter Two

St. Paul's Cathedral

I close my eyes in order to see.
—Paul Gauguin

WITNESSES SAY THAT BEFORE the doors opened to St. Paul's Cathedral in London, the line to get in was a thousand people deep, wrapping around the colossal house of worship. The month was July, the year 2004, and my one-man show of sacred paintings had just been hung. It was displayed directly under the dome of murals, the most sacred holy spot in the cathedral. The murals were created between 1715 and 1719 by court painter Sir James Thornhill and featured scenes from the life of St. Paul. The cathedral is one of London's most famous and recognizable sights. At 365 feet high, its dome is among the highest in the world. It is a church of history and wonder, a tomb of Knights and Royalty, and a sacred place of art and worship. Noted royal weddings have been held there officiated by the Archbishop of Canterbury as the eyes of the world looked on. One of the most noteworthy weddings held there was with Prince Charles and Lady Diana.

Daniel Bonnell

I was one of few painters in history honored with a one-man show at St. Paul's Cathedral. It happened after an Anglican deacon discovered my art. One day during a visit to the US, he walked into my art studio on the third floor of a Victorian mansion owned by an Episcopal Church in Colorado. He loved what he saw and the next thing I knew I had a show in London.

Though most of the visitors were probably tourists, thousands came to St. Paul's every day of the exhibition. A special hardcover book was published describing each painting in the exhibition. Prints were sold. A beautiful four-color brochure was passed out to each viewer in line. It was the best moment of my artistic life, except for one detail. I wasn't there. My wife, Vicki, had just been diagnosed a few days earlier with cancer, and nothing else mattered to me. We came face to face with the trauma monster that knocked on our door day and night, rarely letting us sleep. There was no way I could leave her. Another reason was that I didn't have enough money. The St. Paul show was the biggest show of my life yet, even if Vicki had been in good health, I could not afford a plane ticket.

After the successful show, my paintings were sold and some presented as gifts to various churches and cathedrals around England and the Holy Land. As time went on, well-known authors, theologians, and even a few celebrities from an array of backgrounds recognized my work. However, nothing translated into a financial artistic success.

The next couple of years were the most difficult in the 20-plus years my wife and I had been married. We sold our home in Colorado and moved to an island off South Carolina to be closer to my elderly parents. Vicki and I were both self-employed. I drove around the country selling my art to galleries and shows, making whatever money

I could. Vicki was a psychotherapist and had just a few clients. The sale of our Colorado home gave us a little equity to live on for a few months.

The handwriting was on the wall. By the summer of 2006, money was scarce. With our outrageous health care costs and the rising price of gas forcing me to keep my paintings boxed up instead of on the road, we came to the painful realization that we could not afford to continue doing what we were doing. I reluctantly put down my paintbrushes, bought the trauma monster a drink and went to find some form of a job with medical benefits.

I had never taught before. Never wanted to. Painting was my life. But these were desperate times. I decided to call local schools to see if there were any teaching positions available, a decision that weighed heavily on my brain. While I always saw teaching as a noble profession, it wasn't who I was. But I figured it was one of the few options out there for a starving artist, and something I could do temporarily to earn a living.

I started searching for a teaching job on the island where we lived. Not a single opening existed. My blood pressure skyrocketed. Unless I was going to teach art to a school of fish in the Atlantic, my options were few. I decided to cross the bridge and drift south to Savannah, Georgia. It was 70 minutes away, but I couldn't be picky.

"Yes sir, there is one position open at Beach High School," said a secretary with the Savannah-Chatham County Public School System. "Jackpot!" I thought. I pictured it near the beach, resting along the ocean. I could teach art to energetic students, take a stroll along the beach during my lunch break and make some money doing it. The secretary put me through to the district's human relations director, who asked me if I was certified to teach. Of course I wasn't, but I confidently explained to him my life's work. He didn't care.

"We have several certified candidates to choose from, sorry," he said before hanging up on me. Wait! What? Hello? Was he serious? Not even a conversation? What system was I dealing with? I decided to go straight to the top and wrote a letter to the Superintendent of Education for the State of Georgia.

I wrote that if Matisse could come back from the dead and wanted to teach he would be rejected because he didn't have a teaching certificate. Of course, I'm no Matisse. But wouldn't it be more interesting for an artist to teach art than a teacher to teach art? A week after mailing my letter I received an interview.

Chapter Three

Beginnings

Art is long and life is short, and success is very far off.
—Joseph Conrad

PABLO PICASSO COULD DRAW a dove with one long line while never raising his brush from the canvas. I did the same when signing books that contained my art. I was no Picasso, but the simple symbolic stroke was something that I pursued in my existence, even if fleetingly.

The dove I saw outside the window of my cargo van on a steamy August day in 2006 was one of those few surreal moments life unexpectedly deals you. Picasso's dove was now staring at me and it was no longer a line drawing but the real thing. I was sitting in the empty parking lot of Beach High School, having just arrived for my interview, when the dove landed. In fact, I felt fortunate that I had made it there in one piece. It was in the heart of Savannah's inner city, the most dangerous part of town, and oddly enough it fell into one of the largest National Historic Landmark Districts in America.

Savannah was the first state capital of Georgia and the first planned city in the country. With its majestic oak moss trees and fountains everywhere you look, it has unsurpassable charm and European character. It contains one of the nations earliest cemeteries. Within its iron fences, you will find three signers of the Declaration of Independence, several Europeans killed in duels, and famous artists. Due to its pirate-like romantic European history, Savannah is also known as being the most haunted city in America.

Many staunch Southerners refer to the Civil War as The War of Northern (pronounced naw-thorn) Agression. I refer to it as the war where the South got its butt kicked all the way to the Atlantic and then some. As a result of such an ass-whup'en I think General William Sherman must have had some anger management issues. I figure it came from a Southern belle that stood him up at a West Point Ball, and he never got over the rejection. Why else would he be so pissed off at the South and perform like some pyromaniac, burning down everything in sight? In 1864 Sherman marched into Savannah. After capturing it on that chilly December 22nd evening, he telegraphed President Abraham Lincoln and told him Savannah was his Christmas gift. Sherman chose to save the city from the torch.

Because of Lincoln, the black man's new freedom was born. He promised freed slaves, 40 acres and a mule, but President Andrew Johnson gave the plantation land back to the original owners. It was as if for two hundred years the black man was promised a new beginning with a new home, but when the keys to the house were presented, the house was burned down the night before. Lincoln had freed the black man, then Johnson turned around and placed them in an invisible concentration camp bound by Jim Crow segregation laws and the Ku Klux Klan. There were a recorded 3,400 post Civil War lynchings in the south.[1]

Directly after the war, the first school for children of freed slaves—The Beach Institute—was established. It was named and funded by a famous American inventor, publisher, and patent lawyer named Alfred Ely Beach. Beach also built the first New York City subway in 1860.[2] Why does a rich white guy from the North start the first all black high school in the South? Go figure.

Beach High School today is classified as an at-risk-student school, which means the majority of the students are at risk of dropping out. Beach ranks as one of the worst high schools in the State of Georgia due to its track record of youth-at-risk dropping out and poor test scores. How about this for demographics: the school has over nine hundred students, ninety-eight percent of whom are black; a majority of the kids are from single parent homes with the dads, in most cases, completely absent from their children's lives; about ten percent are homeless, living in shelters or some other form of temporary housing. National statistics show that one out of every three African American male students will be incarcerated before the age of 21.

"What the hell was I doing here?" I asked myself over and over as I sat in the van with the engine running, sucking in the cool air from the vents while killing the fifteen minutes or so that I had left until the interview. My brain was stuck on a loop that had no off switch. This wasn't where I was supposed to be. C'mon, I was a 50-year-old white guy from Hilton Head who painted for a living, sitting in the ghetto of Savannah. It was almost laughable.

As I continued to try and convince myself to put the van in gear and peel out of there, I turned my head to the left and noticed the dove still sitting on the ground next to me. Here I was in the middle of this nowhere, "Dante's Inferno" parking lot, and a white dove was perched near me. I thought for a moment and looked away.

"Okay, get a hold of yourself," I whispered under my breath. "This dove is just hanging out next to me because I must have pulled up on a spot in the lot where his favorite grubs are. Yeah, that's gotta be it."

This was not the first time I had an experience with a dove in this way. A couple of years earlier, I had come home one evening and saw a dove sitting on the apex of my house staring down at me. I knew that it meant I was supposed to be at peace for whatever was coming my way. The next day was when we found out about my wife's breast cancer.

I turned my head away from the window and fiddled with the radio. Out-of-site, out-of-mind, right? I was afraid this dove was another symbol that, once again, I was supposed to be at peace with whatever was coming my way. And I was afraid that what might be headed my way was a job offer at this school that no sane person would ever take. A few minutes later I turned and looked out the window again. There was the dove, tilting his head back and forth, looking at me as if he was expecting me to finish a sentence or something. He obviously wasn't going anywhere. That's when I realized that I needed to not reject the dove, but embrace it.

I turned the engine off, took a deep breath and opened the van door. The dove gently flapped its wings and glided away into the clear blue sky over the school. I went into the building petrified, mystified and eager all at the same time. An hour later I was offered the job. I discovered later that the very spot I saw the dove was where two teachers were almost gunned down by a gang related drive by shooting a few weeks earlier. How's that for symbolism?

As I drove home after my interview that simmering hot August day I decided I needed to cool off, so I stopped to have a beer with a fellow artist in a small nearby town. Bluffton is a community of Lowcountry artists that give it a lot of charm. It's Mayberry with shrimp boats. When I told my friend that I would be teaching art to all black, at-risk kids in the inner city of Savannah his response was, "I would rather have someone staple my tongue to the roof of my mouth before I would do that." As I drove home to tell my wife the news about getting the job my tongue started hurting.

In the Lowcountry there are a lot of flash floods. Rain comes in from off the ocean and for a while you wonder if it will ever stop. The first day of teaching felt like such a flood.

Chapter Four

Diving in Shallow Water

A wise man will make more opportunities than he finds.
—Francis Bacon

I ARRIVED AN HOUR early that first day of teaching. Dressed in a suit, it had to be obvious that I was new. I was probably the only art teacher in the country wearing a suit to art class. Subconsciously I suppose the attire called for respect that revealed my insecurity. Five minutes before class was to begin a scream shot down the hallway from a teacher, "A rat, a rat!" she yelled. I grabbed a custodial broom and ran to her room. Students were streaming in and there was a crowd out in the hall watching through the door window.

I searched for the rat but it was gone. With classes about to begin I quickly pretended I had found and killed the hairy rodent. I then found a plastic bag and pretended to deposit the corpse inside. I substituted a can of air freshener for the volume of the rat inside the bag and then held the bag away from me as I ran out of the classroom and down the stairs to a dumpster. With peace restored I was breathing heavily as I walked back to my class. Upon passing the fearful teacher, whose room was now back in order, she saluted me saying, "You the man Mr. B, you the man!"

Ten minutes passed, I just started my first attendance on the computer and I found myself trying to pronounce my students' names correctly to no avail as I looked out on a sea of black young faces, "Shanequale Demitrous, Quanessa Shaquelle?" I called out hopelessly. Suddenly screams shrieked down the hallway again. Students came running out of the classroom yelling, "rat, and rat rat!" I closed my door and kept on with the roll.

It was then that I made my first big mistake. I called out a name and a response came back, "Yo, I'm here dog." I could tell immediately that this guy was going to put me to the test as he also refused to remove his hat. "I am not your dog!" I firmly yelled back. I then sent him to sit in another part of the room where I could watch him. The rest of the semester he made it his goal to make my life miserable in that first block class. Turns out I deserved it. Everybody but me knew that "dog" in inner city slang meant friend. Clearly, I had a lot to learn.

After the roll I gave a lecture on who I was and why I was there, though not so sure myself; my first students looked at me as dazed as an Amish with an iPhone.

By the end of my first day I had mispronounced 100 names, cleaned up a pint of blood from an uncontrollable nose bleed, stopped a hallway fight, corrected 20 students from not using the F-word, put out a fire in a hallway trash bin, and attempted to kill a rat that was smarter than I was. As the final bell rang all I could hear was a voice in my head that said, "Welcome to the end of your first day of making the biggest mistake of your life."

Chapter Five

Corona Landscapes

If I could find anything blacker than black, I'd use it.
—J. M. W. Turner

IT TAKES A LOT of guts to use black, the anti-color color. All my teachers and professors forbid the use of plain black. Instead we were to use a myriad of other colors that totaled the darkness of black. In order to break the rules you have to first know them, no one knew color better than Turner.

Joseph Mallord William Turner (1775—1851) was an English romantic landscape painter. As you stand before his canvases you are seduced by the use of his color. He painted giant dramatic sunrises and sunsets of an ethereal nature. His art makes you dream. He was a hopeless romantic and his canvases reflected it.

If I used my imagination I could pretend to live in one of his paintings every morning as I traveled to school. It cushioned whatever the day would throw at me.

The time it takes to drive door to door from my house to Beach HS is one hour and ten minutes. Because I have to start teaching at 7:45am, this means I have to leave by 6:00am every morning to clock in and prepare my class. I live on a small island that has no city lights. After all, this is South Carolina, the state that flies the Confederate battle flag over its capital. It is very dark each morning as I drive down lonely two lane roads to the inner city of Savannah, Georgia. I don't mind the drive in complete darkness of night. It makes the drive go faster when you only focus on the headlights in front of you. After an hour the sun starts to rise over the skyline of Savannah just as I cross the Tallmadge Bridge that spans its historic seaport.

As you cross this bridge you climb 185 feet into the air. It is as if you were on a road to heaven itself. On a foggy morning it really feels like you are journeying through the sky. You travel over 1,023 feet with massive cargo ships docked below you and the river traffic of tugboats and ferries that make this an important port in this part of the country.

As you come down the other side, the cityscape of Savannah is waking up to an Eastern sunrise that looks like a Turner painting from start to finish. All that is missing is his signature.

These two lane roads can be dangerous. The temptation to pass a slow moving vehicle can grate on my nerves, however I have been sure to not cave into this temptation. One morning I was coming to work in the pouring rain and a red car quickly sped up to pass both me and the school bus ahead. The red car raced past the school bus on a blind curve and hit an eighteen-wheeler head on. Both the red car and the truck were cruising at 65mph; neither of them had time to hit their breaks.

Soon a police car passed me with his lights and sirens blaring. An ambulance and fire engine do the same. I sat parked there waiting for over an hour behind the school bus on this piece of road that was darker than night itself.

The red lights of the emergency vehicles strangely created a beautiful light show off the wet surface of the road as rain hit the roof of my car. It was a surreal moment. Just ten minutes earlier this guy was alive and well. He just wanted to speed his life up a few seconds. Now he was dead. The dramatic lights of the ambulance brought an exclamation point to the thought.

I never considered myself a drinker. A glass of wine now and then with dinner, a beer or two during the summer was about my limit. I had worked with alcoholics for years in New York City. I knew firsthand the dangers of alcohol.

The drive back home each day seems twice as long as the morning drive. Being stressed that first six months of learning to teach, I would often stop half way and have a Corona at a gas station. It was my reward for making it through another day. It took the anxiety off my nerves just long enough to refocus the balance of the day. I had to get to my studio and paint to deny myself that I was nothing more than a 50 year old babysitter. I found out presumptions can be toxic, a major lesson or pill for me to swallow in the days that followed. Turner, the painter, could help me into Savannah but my Corona stop seemed necessary for my sanity on the road leading home.

Chapter Six

Surreal Fear

We are such stuff as dreams are made on.
—William Shakespeare

When I was age 13, I remember standing before the famous surrealist painting called *The Persistence of Memory* at the Museum of Modern Art in NYC. It was one of Salvador Dali's most famous paintings. He took time and made it soft and fluid, dream-like. Time watches dripping over tree limbs, a woman's closed eye with long lashes in the middle ground of the painting. It was all weird and a bit nuts. This was my first exposure to surrealist art. My first thought was, "This guy's crazy." I did not understand art of the subconscious because I was only 13. It seemed nuts to me that chaos ruled the painting and that I was actually getting in touch with a nightmare within a painting, something I had never expected nor wished. Now, 37 years later, I felt like I was living inside that painting. However the soft clocks had been replaced by school bells, fire alarms, and bomb threats. I was in a walking nightmare thinking I had made the biggest mistake of my life.

Daniel Bonnell

On the second, third, fourth and fifth days of teaching I realized that I had clocked more hours standing in a football field than standing in a classroom. Everyday a student with a cell phone would call in a bomb threat. By law we had to evacuate. The entire school of 900 students and 100 teachers were standing around like pawns on a chess board with no practical moves in front of them. After 30 minutes we would all march to the gym of a middle school some 2 miles away. On many of these marches we were walking in the rain.

Upon arriving at the gym all the students would sit on the bleachers. It only took 15 minutes for the first fight to break out, and then a domino effect took place. One after another fights were breaking out, the dominoes just kept falling. Cops were using their handcuffs like cowboys roping calves in a rodeo. They would lay the students on the floor, jam their knees into thier backs, slap cuffs on them and lead them out. After a couple of hours we would all march back to Beach. As a new teacher I felt like this was some kind of educational hazing initiation, a rite of passage to working in the inner city. However, at the same time, a voice would go off in my head, "Am I nothing but an idiot?" After all, who in their right mind would have the common sense to be standing in these shoes? Every morning that first week I woke up thinking I was living a mistake. I was living in the painting *The Persistence of Memory*[3] where nothing made any sense.

At the end of that first week there was a pep rally planned for the football team. I was not about to go. I had more important priorities to attend to, like making a living to support my family through my painting. So disillusioned was I that I also hung a sign next to my name by my classroom door that read Daniel Bonnell, Visiting Artist. I wasn't willing to make this a long-term commitment. Such apathy set in after a week of this insanity that I thought being fired would be like getting a raise.

In all my 50 years, I had never been called into a principal's office before. It was still an intimidating fear. That following Monday morning the fear came true. The principal's directive was very clear, "Mr. Bonnell you must choose to be a part of the community of this school or not. You will attend every pep rally as a member of this faculty!" I then uncorked my frustrations of what I had witnessed that first week. From no reasonably logical place I dumped my frustration towards this hopeless situation of trying to play catch up with years of educational neglect. "These kids don't know a damn thing about art. They can't even name one artist, dead or alive. They can't name one museum in the world! What have they been learning in art all these years? This is a true crime. The community should know about this. And how can a teacher support a family on this small wage? I have to get home as soon as possible to paint so I can afford to even try to teach!" The principal listened to my illogical defense for skipping out on a pep rally and had nothing else to say except, "We are done here Mr. Bonnell."

Emotionally I was quite a mess. I had become an embarrassment to others and myself. I was embarrassed that at age 50 I had to attend a high school pep rally. Hadn't my life been beyond such a trite activity? At the same time I was an embarrassment to myself because I had not attended but had skipped out like an immature freshman. I was lost in this field of paradox. I had sought out this job but was now running from it. It would take the endurance of a marathon runner to survive.

I now came face to face with my first deficit monster of dozens, all anxiously waiting like an impatient New York deli line. This first foe had only one name—Pride. I was too prideful to go to a pep rally and too prideful to earn a teachers wage. I deserved to be called into the principal's office after all. I had become my biggest obstacle.

By Christmas the bomb threats began to cease. I think the administration realized that every freshman with their first cell phone was going to attempt to get out of a test by calling in a bomb threat. Even the police K9 bomb search dogs were getting bored with the weekly ritual. I was beginning to learn how to run this marathon. Still, I felt like I was lost somewhere in *The Persistence of Memory*. Then my ultimate presumption hit me. Perhaps I died in another life and I was stuck in purgatory with no way out.

Chapter Seven

Four Point Perspective of Four Students

I know of no more encouraging fact than the fact that thought is a sculptor who can create the person you want to be.
—Henry David Thoreau

Jamal

JAMAL WAS A FRESHMAN. He came late to class, sat in the back and usually slept through most of my class. I suppose I didn't blame him. I was after all just learning this teaching shtick and there were days when I put myself to sleep as well. Sometimes I wondered if teaching was mostly a matter of keeping teenagers awake for a full 90 minutes. If I did not make an effort to look for Jamal each day while taking roll, I could have easily counted him absent; he had a natural gift of blending into the wall of the back room.

Several days passed by without Jamal. Then he made his usual unsuspected late appearance to class. "What's your story now, Jamal?" I questioned with a low voice of annoyance. "Jail," he replied. He slowly rolled up his left pants leg to reveal an ankle bracelet. This shiny device allowed the police to monitor his every move. "What is that for?" I said. Jamal looked around to make sure no one could hear him. He then glanced down at the floor quickly and then looked directed at me saying, "Tried to kill my father last week. My younger sister and I sat on a couch hungry as I watched my dad and his girlfriend eat a whole pizza. It wasn't right. My little sister was crying with hunger and I hadn't eaten in two days. So I saw a screwdriver and went at him. I was going to stab his mother fuckin' eyes out. Almost did it too, 'till the cops arrived."

It wasn't long afterwards that Jamal finally received a sure meal every day. Unfortunately this required wearing an orange jump suit with "Chatham County Jail" plastered on his back.

Shanequa

There are a lot of Lowcountry cultural laws of nature. One of those laws is arriving to an appointment, church, dinner, or school at least 30 minutes beyond the designated time. I once had an appointment with a black pastor for 10am. After waiting for 45 minutes he finally arrived, with no apology for being late. It appears my students were all on Lowcountry time. One of those culturally stuck students was Shanequa. She would drag in late each morning and her head would hit the desk like the gavel of a constipated judge.

One day I asked Shanequa to stay after class. "What is going on with you?" I asked with a frustrated affect. "Mista B, I work from 7-ta-3am every day to support me mother.

Please don't fail me. My dad left her and me when I was 3 and he comes around now-n-then to rob us."

I had Shanequa come to my class at lunchtime to eat her food and do her make-up art every day. I also had four other students who came back to my class after getting their lunch simply because they felt safer there than eating in the lunch room. The art room had become a safe haven. Shanequa would down her lunch in one minute, do five minutes of an art assignment and then, bam! Her head would hit the desk for 20 more minutes of lustful sleep.

That Friday afternoon Shanequa stood up to read a poem she wrote in the student talent contest before the whole school. The poem was called, *Why I Hate My Father*. She received a standing ovation; apparently she was not alone with this emotion.

She wrote another poem and let me keep it. It is entitled In a Box.

> In a box
> A dark one, dark inside no light
> From the sun
> Scream and shout. I can't get out
> But nobody hears like me, no body cares.
>
> In a box
> Slowly losing air, about to go insane
> Pulling out chunks of my hair.
> Body cramped-up-so now I'm stiff.
> In a box.
> Trapped.

Taz

Drug raids are common at Beach High. The students were intuitive about them. They knew when one was about to go down. It was as if someone blew a whistle or pulled a warming alarm that only at-risk-teens could hear. Sure enough, the principal would come over the loud speaker, "Teachers, lock your doors and do not allow any student out of your room!" Then a bang would resound from the door; it was always a cop knocking roughly. After a quick announcement of their intention they herded all the students out into the hallway to be searched while a German shepherd dog would sniff out the room for drugs.

On one specific Tuesday, just prior to one of these raids I noticed an extra student in my class. It was Taz. He had a way of showing up when he wanted to and he always reeked of weed. Today Taz had a problem; students were dropping all around him, getting high off his fumes alone! I quickly grabbed his weed-smelling jacket and stashed it in a back storeroom up high and out of sight. I only hoped that the dog would not be allowed into the back room.

Fortunately, the cops never even opened the storeroom door. The day was saved. Just recently, I was cleaning out my back closet and found Taz's jacket still crammed in a corner on the top shelf. "What-the-hell," I said to myself —and there it remains still smelling of weed.

Taz would often show up in my room unexpectedly, long after I had called the roll. I had a long chat with him one day to understand why. I discovered a secret I will never forget.

His mother was raped. She kept the baby and told him that his father was a demon. She convinced him he had no natural father. This baby was Taz. He had defined himself as the son of a demon. His whole personality was developed around this belief, and as a result referred to himself as the Tasmanian Devil, or Taz for short.

Jermaine

Jermaine was a junior the first year that I taught. He was almost seven feet tall but he hated basketball. Jermaine was one of those students who loved to chill in my room during lunch. He and three other guys would sit in the back of the room and forgo eating lunch all together. I later discovered that not every student received a free lunch, only those whose parents were at the poverty level or below. Many students, therefore, starved each day because their parents could not afford to give them any money for lunch or could not afford to pack a lunch. I also learned later that many students hated their summers because the hot school lunch was often the only time they would ever eat.

Jermaine and his friends would sit in the back of the class and shoot dice, laugh and tell jokes, pull out porno, and show each other comic art that they drew. I turned my back on all of it but would occasionally tell them to cut the profanity. One day I asked to see one of the comic strips they were passing around. Jermaine was excited to show me his art! He handed me several pages of loose-leaf paper that was drawn as well as a professional DC comic artist. It was a story about a young black man who got his brains blown out by a gang. I was told that the dead youth was based on Jermaine's brother, who was shot right in front of him that summer during a gang fight gone wrong. Drawing the images realistically helped Jermaine cope with the pain and loss that he did not know how to express. I bought the comic strip from Jermaine for $20. It is the most valuable piece of art I own.

Jermaine barely graduated from Beach. His three other friends went into the army. I often saw Jermaine just walking around his enighborhood alone, still looking for a safe place.

Chapter Eight

Rhythm

Movement is the soul of all things.
—Auguste Rodin

ONE OF THE MOST controversial compositions of the twentieth century in music was written by John Milton Cage,[4] (1912—1992) an American composer, philosopher, poet, music theorist, artist, and printmaker. Cage's composition was simply silence. He sat at the piano motionless for four minutes and 33 seconds while the audience was to listen to simply the sounds of their environment.

John Cage's art is always visually balanced and there is a flow of energy and rhythm that does not stop. Rembrandt did this with his portraits of beautiful women. His highlights always keep your eyes moving in a never-ending triangle. From the highlight on a pearl, hanging in the center of a woman's forehead to the two highlights in each of her eyes—one's eyes keep moving. The same pattern occurs with his nudes—but I will leave that up to your own imagination. Van Gogh's Starry Night is a pure flow of energy with short and long brushstrokes flowing in spiral jetties in the sky, with a classic post-impressionistic movement of the brush. Even quantum physics has revealed to us that all matter is actually moving at the speed of light, proving that the universe itself is one giant flow of energy as rhythm.

Rhythm is usually predictable. It has a pattern or has structure to it. Rhythm hardly ever attended Beach High School but energy sure did.

At Beach High School the energy is such that you had better be attentive, because it is always coming right at you from every direction. You might get hit right between the eyes with it, in the back of the head, or it might roll right over you like a monster truck in Yazoo, Mississippi. It would probably be wise for teachers to wear helmets during instruction.

Usually it's a gangster hip-hop form of energy that starts early in the morning down the hall from me. On one particular day, the beat started earlier than usual. There was a male teacher, mid 40's, black, and a seasoned educator. A male student provoked him. Profanity echoed off the cheap ceiling tiles and leaked into the surrounding rooms. This teacher picked the student up and body slammed him against the wall. Both the teacher and the student were suspended from school and a whole instruction period was lost for 3 days.

Downstairs it was the first day for a new veteran French teacher. He quit at the end of the day exclaiming, "These students are un-teachable." He handed his letter of resignation to the front secretary without even looking her in the eye. According to Dr. Heather Bilton, who works for the Education Department in Georgia, sixty percent of all new teachers in this district mail in their keys by Thanksgiving break.

A third wave of unbalanced, John Cage compositional energy built like a tsunami at the furthest end of the second floor. A respectable, white, older history teacher pulled a male student out into the hall yelling, "We're going to have a coming to Jesus meeting right now!" The next year this teacher retired. By now the energy started smoking-literally- as we witnessed a fire lit in a trashcan. The arriving police couldn't find a designated fire extinguisher, because it was stolen. The smell of burnt rubber hung in the air the whole day.

On the first floor a student had her cell phone taken away from her by an assistant principal. "Fuck it!" the student yelled out as she took her phone and slammed it against the wall, leaving it in a pile of plastic and micro chips on the floor. The student had been waiting to receive a message to know if her mother had died that day of AIDS.

The crescendo came as the school's blaring alarm sounded, signaling an evacuation. Some student called in a bomb threat so that he wouldn't have to take an exam that was planned for the next 90 minutes. The whole school had to evacuate everyone and 900 students and faculty stood in a football field, again, soaked by an unexpected Lowcountry rain. What next? Fire engines and police cars raced to the scene and surround the school.

That afternoon, after the last bell had rung, I turned out the lights in my room. I sat there staring towards the furthest end of my classroom as a welcomed natural light calmed the room like a giant hug or a soft kiss as it flowed through the tall windows. For one second I thought I saw John Cage sitting in the back of my classroom in silence, observing the composition of the day; he laughed and disappeared.

Chapter Nine

Special Needs Saints

Have the humble attitude—to see things simply is the hardest thing in the world.
—Charles Hawthorne

JOHN WAS THE ONLY white student in a class of 20 special needs students. He came in as a new student my second year of teaching. I loved my special needs kids because they defined a new existence of innocence for me. One day I overheard John shatter that cloak of innocence while conversing with another special needs teen, wondering what it would be like to f*** a woman. His fellow students had no idea what he was talking about. I was furious. I called John out into the hallway and explained to him how inappropriately he was behaving. Truth is, I was mad as hell at him and regretted him disrupting the class I believed to be so innocent. It even made me mad that he was white.

That afternoon I had time to sit with my emotions, which were now down from a boil to a simmer. John was several notches higher in intelligence than the rest of the class, and I had cursed him for being so. He was not bright enough to be mainstreamed into other classes. He had tried over and over and failed over and over again. Finally John felt in control on a level he had never known before. He was in a special needs class that accepted him and one in which he excelled, though it was quite slow in every manner.

John was a pain in the ass and he drove me nuts. He also drove paraprofessionals crazy. He just didn't fit anywhere. As I would teach a class, John would be looking down and talking to himself under his breath. Eventually he could not control his need for rest and would sleep every class away.

I called his mother. I told her about the inappropriate language and behavior and that it had to stop. On the end of the phone I could hear a desperate mom begging, "Oh, Mr. Bonnell, please, please, please, John is happy for the first time in his life. For the first time he looks forward to going to school every day. He dresses himself and waits eagerly for the bus to come. For the first time he has a life. He has an older brother that tells him horrible things and that is where he gets this behavior from. He has no father and I have to work all day and I have to entrust him to his older brother. Please, oh please give him another chance."

Where I had made John out to be a jackass I now realized that I was the jackass. John was just being human. He just didn't have the tools to manage his life due to a mental illness. He was a teen who dreamed of just being normal. His hormones spoke louder than his ability to control his mouth.

When I could see past my frustration, I realized that John was quite an artist. He could follow every assignment perfectly and always beat the other students to finishing the simple work. One day I asked the class if they knew of any animal that we read about that is not real. I was thinking of a unicorn and hoping others would think the same thing. No one could recall any make believe animal, not even Big Bird, a dragon or Barney. After a long, long silence John lifted his head up off his desk as if coming out of a coma, 'A Pegasus', he said, promptly putting his head back down. "Excuse me?" I said. "Was that you John?" His head rose up one more time, "A Pegasus, Mr. Bonnell, it's a winged horse."

I went to the computer, having never heard of such a word. I googled Pegasus and sure enough, John was correct. I was ecstatic. "John you are soooooo right!" I yelled out. I went crazy in the classroom as if John had won the lottery. "You have taught this 54 year old man a new word, thank you, thank you, thank you." I had all the other students applaud him. For the first time in his life someone recognized John. For the first time someone other than his mother and his crude brother saw him. Until then he had been invisible.

Two weeks later John's desk sat empty for many days. I wondered if he was just ill, but eventually I went to find someone who could tell me what had happened to John.

"John's in an asylum," said a special needs administrator. She continued, "Turns out all his sleeping spells and talking with himself revealed he is schizophrenic." Now John has nothing but a life of living in an institution that confirms to him day after day that he has a problem that defies him ever having a normal life.

Suddenly his past outburst to a fellow male student months earlier of, "Hey, do you think we will ever know what it is like to F*** a woman?" became real, human, normal and anything but crude. What a jackass I was—not John. Perhaps if I can visit John I can break his illusion that life is only his illness, and I can break my own chronic illusions of presumption.

Chapter Ten

Pastor Blade

You cannot express yourself with a language that is chaotic.

—Kimon Nicoliades

PABLO PICASSO SOUGHT A primitive style of art.[5] Pretentious, contrived art was out and primitive beauty was in. He turned to the art of Africa and discovered it in a fetish of African masks. I was well acquainted with this form of art from the Dark Continent.

The best year of my life was when I lived in remote villages of Africa in 1982. One of the greatest value lessons I learned came from a humble African farmer in Ghana. I stopped him one day in the middle of harvesting his crops to ask for directions. He was patient with me and spent time asking me questions about who I was, where I came from and the like. In fact, he clearly would have stood there all day long talking with me with great unselfish focus. I learned right away that people are more important than time in Africa. Africans taught me that the time you give to another person will come back to you. To cut a conversation short is to cheat yourself out of valuable time later.

How far removed was this principle from the American value system. Here was the upside down principle working at its best.

After I had survived my first six months at Beach High School I found a new friend that understood this value. His name is Pastor Blade. I first met him when I visited the ISS Class (In School Suspension). He was the head of ISS, which meant he had a pain-in-the-ass job for 8 hours, babysitting students that were too lazy to go to class or were busted for fighting, etc. I visited the class once to give a student some make up work. As I approached his classroom door from the hall I could hear him, loud and clear, directing a student, "Get your fat male-hoe-ass in that chair and get your work done!" Yes, I did say he is a pastor. It might sound highly unorthodox but his students knew that he cared for them. One has to keep in mind in this demographic that virtually none of these students have a father at home.

At times I would seek him out to act as a reality checker for me, a white naïve new teacher who was clueless about the cross cultural dynamics of teaching within an all black at-risk-high school. Just like the African farmer that took time for me in Ghana, so would Pastor Blade.

One day after school I had had enough of this teaching gig. Some days you feel like a baby sitter in a detention center for messed up youth. You have days where you fall flat on your face. The next thing you know you hear the monster of regret knocking at your door and he's yelling, "I told you so, you dumb-ass, thinking that you could teach?!?!"

So this one particular day I had sat down with Pastor Blade in his class. He ran his students out of the room and locked the door so we could talk privately. For the next

15 minutes I dumped on him how impossible it is to be a parent, peacekeeper, sheriff and the stress of rarely finding the time to even teach in between.

Pastor Blade then sat up more erectly, his eyes locked into mine, staring like a million dollar Las Vegas poker face. Then he spoke, "When Jesus told Peter, 'Get behind me Satan,' what do you think he was really saying?" That was easy, I expounded on the vision of Jesus towards Jerusalem and His destiny with the cross and all that laid before him in the coming hours in the garden of Gethsemane. I went on to break down the human element of Peter simply trying to protect his master, thinking that he knew what was best for him like some presidential bodyguard.

After I proudly delivered my deep theological exegesis to Pastor Blade I looked up to see him put his head in his hands and exclaim, "Lord, we have sooo much work to do with this man!" He then looked me right in the eye and said. "Mr. Bonnell, will you permit me to use my inner city language in this matter?" "Sure Pastor," I said with a perplexed look. Then once again he locked his gaze into mine. "What he was saying was not "Get behind me Satan," but "Satan kiss my ass!"

I must confess that it took a moment to sink in, kind of like feeling that after burn when you take a shot of Jack Daniels on a cold, below freezing, winter day. The after burn is what it's all about. Class dismissed.

Chapter Eleven

The Invisible

The soul is dyed the color of its thoughts.
—Marcus Aurelius Antoninus

Rene Magritte was a Belgian painter[6] (1898–1967) that was known for his illusionary works of art. One of his paintings that best represents his creative thinking process is that of a man looking into a mirror only to see the back of his head instead of his face. It is an image of being lost, a stranger to one's self. In fact, there is not even a title to the painting.

On March 12, 1912, Magritte's mother committed suicide. She drowned herself in a river. She had made many attempts over the years to kill herself, driving her husband to lock her into her bedroom. On that dark day in March she escaped, and was missing for days. Her body was found a mile down the river, dead. According to the story, 13-year-old Magritte was present when her body was pulled from the river. When his mother was found, her dress was covering her face. It was an image that has been used as the source of several of his paintings depicting loss.

Being involved in my students' lives sometimes means witnessing the invisible child. It means witnessing loss. They are not seen by anyone. They have no validation of even being human. Like Magritte's mother, no one recognizes them. In time they don't recognize themselves. I had never known such suffering existed.

Sitting in the waiting room of the Chatham County Jail reminded me of sitting at the Department of Motor Vehicles holding a ticket for the next in line. Only it somehow felt dangerous to be sitting there. There were two long rows of bolted down chairs, a flat screen TV on a far wall with news on, and a big center desk against the back wall. Behind the desk sat a pleasant looking woman. She knew her stuff. She patiently managed a queue of people 10 deep seeking to be processed by her so that they could visit their husbands, relatives, sons, daughters, and friends.

It was the first time I had ever visited a jail. I thought the whole idea was to avoid the place, so I had done a good job for 54 years until now. "I'd like to visit Jamal Wilson," I said, as I handed her my driver's license. "What's the nature of your visit?" she asked. "Former teacher," I said. She told me to take a seat and expect a 20-minute wait. As I sat there listening to the nauseating bias swill of the TV news station blaring in my ears, two little children around the ages of three and four started fighting and crying. They would stop briefly and then fight and cry some more. I could not think of a more depressing place to be.

Sitting there I could not help but think that this place was an ad for Harley Davidson Motorcycles. Tattoos, hats and shirts displayed this biker icon: vagabond, greased back hair, and sun burned skin. There is a trophy case in the waiting area. Now, that is weird when you think about it, a trophy case, with sharp shooting trophies all lined up.

I suppose it is a determent if some visitor wants to come packing a gun.

"Visitor for Wilson!" the desk cop called out. I quickly placed all my known metal objects on her desk and walked through the metal detector. The alarm went off loudly anyway. She laughed and handed me back my personal items and said, "Go ahead, take the first right down the hall, he is sitting under a sign labeled C1."

After going through a mystery door that had warning labels posted all over it I found myself walking down a long white hall the length of a football field with no windows. The mother and the two little girls that had been fighting earlier were now walking ahead of me. The girls laughed and ran down this hall like it was routine to them, and it probably was.

As I walked up to the visiting station I felt like I was in a zoo for humans painted in institutional green paint. Rather than viewing a lion through bars, I was viewing a human being through one inch thick bulletproof glass. A swivel stool swung out and I sat uncomfortably for 20 minutes trying to have a conversation through a mini speaker on the table. Jamal stood there as if he was about to leave. He did not know who his visitor was. He bit his lip and kept looking down at the floor and then sat down. "Remember me Jamal?" I asked. With his head down he nodded yes.

It had been a while since I'd seen Jamal. I recall the first time I saw him in my class. He sat alone in my room all by himself, far away from his peers. Every time I called out his name while taking role he would only raise his hand; he would never call out, "present". It was days later that I discovered he was a self-mute, meaning he could talk but he chose not to.

One day I sat next to Jamal after I got the class going on a project that involved discovering your best signature. I pulled out a piece of paper for him to write on. "Jamal, I know something bad must have happened to you many years ago and that's why you have chosen to not talk, am I right?" I said, quietly, so others could not hear me. He took his pencil and wrote, "Yes." "What happened, Jamal?" I asked.

With the handwriting of a second grader he wrote out the word, SEX. "Was this done by a relative?" I asked. Jamal scribbled out the letters DAD. "How old were you?" He stared at the floor refusing to look me in the eye. He slowly wrote out the number 6. His father had performed some unspeakable sexual act on this innocent boy, which caused him to emotionally implode. The trauma of the act, of the experience, turned him into a mute. I can imagine his father yelling something to the effect of, "And you better never tell anyone about this or I'll fucking kill you!" Fear gave birth to Jamal's silence for life.

I then took Jamal's signature and taught him how to sign his name in such a manner that it would become a power signature like Michael Jordon or Serena Williams. I taught him to see himself as an important person in this world and that your signature need not be a lie but a focal point that you live towards, that having a signature that reveals good self esteem is a great thing. After rewriting his signature several times and creating a dynamic symbol out of his first and last name I placed his new signature in front of him and said, "Here Jamal, this is your new signature." He studied the signature for the longest time and slowly a smile came over his face. Though he struggled to do so, he practiced writing his new signature for a good while. Then I gave Jamal a job I thought he could do as a personal favor to me. "Jamal, see those hundreds of books along the wall? Do you think you could place them in some kind of order so they were in neat piles for me? This would be a great favor to me," I explained.

Thirty minutes later, before the bell was to ring, I glanced over at Jamal having forgotten I had asked him to do me a favor. He was sitting proudly at his desk working on his new signature and I was shocked by what I saw. Each book was placed in perfect order in stacks that could pass any Marine inspection. I was proud of him and let him know it.

One week later Jamal didn't come back to class. He had been arrested and was in jail. That was the last time I saw him, until a year later.

I decided to go find Jamal. I felt I had to find him. He was lost and someone needed to seek after him. I had no idea what I would do when I found him but I would cross that bridge when I came to it.

I finally found Jamal. He was in the Chatham County Jail being held without bail. A day before his incarceration he had walked into a Target store and pulled out a knife. He was using the knife to jimmy a lock that held iPods. He got caught by a security guard and wrestled with him. Jamal took away the guard's gun and pointed it at him but was tackled by three other guards from the back. Because he was "mute" he didn't utter a word.

I only visited Jamal twice in jail. Of course I did all the talking. I wanted him to know that I saw him, that he is a valuable person. I made him look me in the eyes while I affirmed his worth in this life that I see him. He is not invisible. I told him I would come visit him in a week if he promised to talk to me. He nodded yes. I explained to him that he could not defend himself or help himself if he chose to remain silent the rest of his life. There was too much life wanting to get out but he had to let himself free from his chains.

The next week I kept my promise. I was right on time to this human zoo. "You promised to talk with me Jamal, you promised." I was only allotted 20 minutes to visit. It was the longest 20 minutes of silence in my life. Jamal was a soul who was lost too far down the river to ever surface again. He had drowned when he was 6 years old.

That night after my last visit with Jamal I had a nightmare. Like Rene Magritte I discovered a dead body a mile down river; only instead of a dress pulled up over a face it was an inmate's shirt. Upon removing the shirt it was the face of Jamal.

There exist thousands of invisible youth in our high schools. No one knows who they are, no one sees them until it is too late, until they are seen behind a glass wall in a county jail or after they are pulled from a river having committed suicide.

Artists show themselves and others something they've never seen before, even if it's painful, to put a face on the invisible—like Jamal.

Chapter Twelve

The Hidden Masterpiece

Art seems to me to be a state of soul, more than anything else.
The soul of all is sacred.
—Marc Chagall

THERE EXISTS A VERY small painting of greatness in the Met. It is in one of those hidden places near the impressionist section, lurking in the shadows. The painting is called The Laundress by the French painter, Honre Daumier.[7] You could easily walk right by it and never notice it. The painting is simple and yet complex. As the sun is about to set, a mountain of a woman with a large basket of clothes under her left arm holds her daughter by her right hand. She and her daughter have climbed long stairs up from the Seine River in Paris. The colors depict amber, yellow and blue hues reflecting the emotional end of a long, hard day. The well-defined curves of the muscles on the mother reveal backbreaking work, strength, and the conditioning of a hard life. Where words leave off, painting picks up: a sort of visual poetry. The heart of the painting is found in seeing beauty and dignity within simplicity, hidden in the shadows.

Many students at Beach High School reflect such painful dignity as Daumier's, *The Laundress*. They are students that never knew their biological father, yet they survived never having a daddy to worship as a child. Though only teenagers they are determined human beings that hold down jobs at night to help their mothers make ends meet come the end of each month. They are often quiet and misunderstood. Most of their peers show no respect to authority, but not these kids. They bust their butts and beat all odds of survival, yet retain a quiet contentment with life and the cards that were dealt them. Such youth like this never make the news; they don't have criminal records. One of these young students is Alicia. I had Alicia right after B lunch in my advanced art class. She always made sure she had a smile upon greeting me and always asked me how my day had gone. She always did her work and made an effort to knock the assignment out of the ballpark. She also had a malignant brain tumor.

Alicia had undergone so many surgeries that radiation had stolen most of her hearing. Still, she never complained about not hearing an assignment and chose to not wear any hearing aid, because it would make her feel out of place with the rest of the class. She was a straight A student and asked me almost weekly how my wife's breast cancer recovery is going.

Just like that hidden corner within the Met Museum where thousands of people never see the treasure before them, so exists the Alicia's of our world.

Alicia has no father. She takes care of her special needs younger brother while her mother holds down two jobs. Like the elegant strength found in Daumier's The Laundress, so Alicia's life reflects the same determined, resolute power of character.

Chapter Thirteen

Castles in the Sky

Art is a step in the Known toward the unknown.
—Kahlil Gibran

ONE DAY IN ART school, back when I was in my twenties, a guest artist showed the class a series of photos he had made called *Castles in the Sky*. I was quite touched by them. In New York City the buildings tower so high that you feel like you're in a canyon. You only feel sunshine around noon each day because it is only then when the sun can peak through these mountains made of concrete, metal, iron and glass. This guest artist explained to us how he took his camera out into the center of the street and shot scene after scene of half sky and half buildings. They were nothing special, just skyscrapers and sky, boring stuff actually, until he did one thing with them—he turned them upside down. When upside down the sky transformed the buildings. Suddenly the sky resembled a castle.

In the teachings of Jesus he was always turning things upside down. He was the upside down teacher. His disciples never understood; most Christians still don't get it today. "Blessed are the poor..," he would evoke. "Love your enemies and pray for those that persecute you," he would command. "To be the greatest you must be the servant of all," he would tell his followers as he washed their feet. His most upside down remark was, "To gain your life you must lose it for my sake."

As a wanna-be follower, what would that mean to me today, 2,000 years after Jesus taught such radical teachings? Such a drastic approach to walking through life is, after all, un-American. In this country we play to win. We are into "shock-and-awe", demonizing political parties, and working for the American dream. Americans are into winning at all costs. This talk about the first shall be last is unheard of in such a winner-takes-all capitalist society.

I think of those boring (when viewed right side up) cityscape photos back in art school and see that those are actually photos of you and me. Those are images of our illusions of success and the good life. Those are our perceptions that become our realities in a self-absorbed world. So I decided to sell out. To sell out to this upside down perception that Jesus called the Kingdom of God.

For me this meant to be standing in the most impossible place I could be, to turn my life upside down at a school called Beach.

I chose the castles in the sky.

Chapter Fourteen

The Question

Knowledge comes, but wisdom lingers.
—Alfred Lord Tennyson

FEAR. RACE. KLAN. ROPE. Hate. Kill. The brain thinks in concrete images and often revolves around four letter words. Each of these words immediately denotes an image of racism, burning crosses, death and suffering. The renowned painter Philip Guston[8] once spoke as a visiting artist to my art school back in the seventies. He showed his latest work, which was being rejected by the critics. They were paintings of him wearing a KKK hood painting a portrait of a Klansmen. His intended statement was that all of us are prejudice in some form or manner.

There is a form of prejudice in America; black men are still slaves, but to statistics. One of those statistics is that one out of every three black men will be incarcerated before the age of 21. Why is this? I posed this question to my class one morning.

I held up a bag of Snickers bars and said, "Whoever can stand up and tell the class the reason why one out of three black men will be incarcerated before the age of 21 gets rewarded." Suddenly a sea of hands shot up. A female student named Clarissa abruptly stood up and exclaimed, "They goes to jail cuz they ain't got no fuckin' daddy at home!"

I hate the F-word. I hear it a hundred times a day and correct students until I feel like I was the F-word cop, but today I would have needed to call a back up squad to prevent it. Then a student named Shandra stood up and yelled at her across the room "You don't know what the fuck you're talkin' 'bout! I never grew up with any fuck'en daddy and I turned out just fuckin' fine!" "That's what the fuck you think!" came a hidden voice from the back of the class. "Fuck you!" yelled Clarissa with a vengeance. Laughter fell like a torrential Lowcountry downpour of rain. A large male student named Dante stood up and demanded his right to speak on the subject. "Truth be told Mr. Bonnell, all of us can buy drugs any time day or night. Half of the male students in this class are dealing. So sooner or later they will get their fuckin' butts busted and put into jail. Then when they get out-a-here and no college will accept them they just deal more until they get caught over and over. It's all fucked up. When all else fails then you just join the army and take your chances." "Shit no!" came another male voice. "I ain't joinin' no fuckin' army!" yelled another student. " Mr. Bonnell! I will tell you the fuckin' answer to your question. It's cuz their daddy's never taught them shit cuz they wasn't around and their mothers was on welfare or had a live-in boyfriend or cuz they was living with ten brothers and sisters from three different daddies who never married their fucking mother!"

Suddenly there was a surprising lull of silence amid the loud chaos of voices when a male student, who was also in a gang, said, "This is like one of those moments in them fucking teacher movies where the white teacher changes the lives of all his students in one magical moment." Upon laughing out loud no one could hear me because the bell rang to change classes, suddenly one student grabbed my bag of Snickers and threw them all into the air. Students were scrambling like starving pigeons after the candy. Thirty seconds later every one was gone. The class fell into silence. I sat there for a long five minutes, and then pulled a saved Snickers out of my shirt pocket. I ate each bite slowly, and muttered to myself—"F'in good candy bar."

Chapter Fifteen

The Kitten

The supreme happiness of life is the conviction that we are loved.

—Victor Hugo

It was the best piece of art to come out of Hollywood in decades. It was one of the momentous moments in film. In the mid-seventies the country stood around the coffee machines at work talking about it. It was *One Flew Over the Cuckoo's Nest*.

At the end of the movie Chief Broom surprises everyone. For most of the movie everyone is led to believe that he is deaf and dumb in this hospital for the insane, this "cuckoo's nest". The Chief turns to his close friend McMurphy and has a conversation for the first time in 10 years by saying, "It wasn't me that started acting deaf; it was people that first started acting like I was too dumb to hear or see or say anything at all."

Chief Broom is a massive Native American and he towers over everyone with an intimidating presence. He believes he is extremely weak in spite of his Hulk-like body. In the last scene he recovers his personal strength and escapes from the hospital by throwing a sink through a wall to bust out. This breaking through the wall was symbolic of his breaking the illusion built by others. Buying into the perceptions that others have of you can be toxic and deadly.

Arnold is one of my special needs students that reminded me of Chief Broom. He was new to the class. In the first week of school he would come in with the class casting a huge shadow on the rest of us. With a neck as thick as a watermelon and shoulders as wide as a refrigerator, he would dwarf anyone who sat next to him. Unlike all the other special needs students in the class, Arnold would sit perfectly still with his hands flat on the table in front of him. His brow was so large he looked like an angry, massive Russian that was one move away from being crushed in a game of chess. His demeanor would never change nor his statue-like frozen state. When called upon Arnold would slightly move his massive head as if it were mechanical in order to see me.

It was only the second day of the new school year. Arnold was new to the special needs class. The other 16 students along with myself had grown to become a sort of pseudo family. Arnold was welcomed with open arms by all.

I began the class by pointing to a mural of famous African Americans and asking the class if they knew who they were. Arnold raised his hand. "Yes, Arnold, do you know the answer?" I asked. "Martin Luther King, Jr." Arnold uttered quietly. The class applauded unselfishly. I then pulled out several Beach Bucks, which I use as an in house currency redeemable for stuffed animals, used TV's and more. The student's eyes got huge, and you could hear exciting exclamations of "wow" everywhere. I exclaimed,

"Arnold if you can tell me the name of the most famous speech that Martin Luther King Jr. gave I will give you 10 Beach Bucks right now!" A large silence fell over the class. Shannon, who was sitting at the end of the room grabbed her washcloth to catch her excessive drooling, somehow her smile grew even larger. She leaned forward and said, "Ooooh Weeeeee!"

Arnold sat thinking. I gave him a full minute to answer and said, "Time's up!" Arnold replied, "Can you repeat the question?" I repeated the question and all eyes were implanted on Arnold in great hope. "I have a dream speech," he said. The class went nuts. Shannon wiped her mouth again and screamed in joy. Others stood up and applauded as if they had heard Beethoven for the first time. I counted out 10 Beach Bucks and the class counted out each one with me. Arnold sat motionless as always. I raised the bar. "Arnold, I am so proud of you that I will give you another question for ten more Beach Bucks. Can you tell me the name of the monument that was behind Martin Luther King Jr. that day?" I said.

The moment was something out of a scene from *Who Wants to be a Millionaire?* My class had to be calmed down. This time, Arnold took a full five minutes to think. "Times up," I said. Arnold turned his head ever so slightly and this time actually looked at me and said once more, "Can you repeat the question?" Now in the drama of the moment it was as if Arnold represented the whole class. If Arnold answered the question correctly and showed himself to be mindfully intelligent then everyone was mindfully intelligent, even for just a 90 minute period on a Tuesday morning in September in the inner city of Savannah, Georgia.

The sad dynamic about special needs students is that they are aware that most of them have mental and physical limitations. They are helpless victims from birth, always being redirected and corrected. The gift in this existence, from my vantage point, is that each of them is accepting of themselves and each other, something that has been my own mental disability my whole life. These saints in waiting do not compare and contrast each other to themselves. Therefore they do not experience jealousy, malice or envy like the rest of us do. The writer Christian Bobin writes about one of the secrets of Saint Francis: ". . . nothing can be made known about the most high except through the most low."

"Time's up!" I said. Silence crashed, eyes froze, breathing stopped. "Lincoln?" said Arnold. "Yes!" I screamed, "It was Lincoln!!" The class broke into joyful elation and stood up cheering their new hero. Arnold sat still and frozen as always without even a smile. I kept wondering what was going on in his internal being. Perhaps he was joyfully experiencing our acknowledgement of his intelligence. Perhaps there was very little at all. I then told Arnold that he could go to the back of the room and pick out any stuffed animal that he wished for the twenty Beach Bucks he had earned. Another teacher took him by the hand and led him to the small school store that I had set up for students to spend their Beach Bucks. The store contained over 200 stuffed animals of all sizes. Arnold made his selection and returned to his desk. I continued with the daily lesson plan. Ten minutes later one of the other teachers directed my attention toward Arnold again. Arnold had chosen a small stuffed animal kitten that was black and white. He sat there, actually moving for once. He was stroking the kitten gently non-stop as if it had been deprived of love its whole life.

Shadow Lessons

When I saw Arnold caressing his chosen gift I realized that something special had just happened. All of us saw a side of Arnold that was the opposite of how he appears. I thought of the quote from Chief Broom stating, "It wasn't me that started acting deaf; it was people that first started acting like I was too dumb to hear or see or say anything at all." Within this intimidating large teenager was a gentle and kind human being that was not embarrassed to love out loud, even stroking a stuffed animal.

That afternoon as I was driving back to the island in my van, the usual dark monster of regret and depression sat in the passenger seat next to me. I had only $80 left in my checking account. How was I going to pay my bills that month? What if I ran out of gas before getting home? My van had over 200,000 miles on it and I was still making payments. When would one of my paintings sell next?

I stopped at a gas station to buy a beer and sat in my van reflecting on Arnold and what had happened to him that morning. I knew that evening when he got home and his mother asked him how his day had gone he would have something special to share with her. His life had changed that day. I saw him stroking his kitten that he now owned, which he had earned, which he now loved. I finished my Corona and tossed the bottle. Now I had only $78 in my checking account, but who the hell cared?

Chapter Sixteen

The Boss

Don't try to learn a formula, but to become sensitive, to feel deeply.
—Kimon Nicoliades

ROMANTICISM[9] WAS AN ART movement born in 1790 and went into a coma in 1850. On occasion she comes out of her coma and the world gets some great art, then she goes back to sleep again. Romanticism embraced emotion over reason and the senses above the intellect. This is a good definition of a special needs child, one who always values emotion over reason, and acknowledges the senses to be better than the intellect.

I admit it. I confess it. I'm a romantic. I feel too much. It gets me into trouble all the time. I even turn chaos and madness into a form of romanticism. I guess that is how I survive most moments of my reality.

One insane reality of working within an at-risk high school is that if the school does not progress with graduating a certain quota of seniors each year or meet certain test score levels then the school gets its budget slashed. Bad performance means all the money goes elsewhere—to other schools. For an art teacher, who has no bearing on such statistics, this means you have no budget for any supplies. It is at those moments you want to quit. It's like being a carpenter with no hammer or a lighthouse in a desert.

Art, music and theatre are not on the map in public schools. Accept it or leave it.

One who teaches such an art form must decide to embrace the blindness and the madness of the system, or just run off. It's kind of like buying the monster of ignorance a drink during happy hour. To want to work within such a bubble of naiveté is madness. I choose to remain in the madness even though I feel like I am only mopping the deck of the Titanic as the lifeboats are being lowered. I learned how to swim at an early age so I figure I have a good back up plan. That's the stupid romantic in me.

Due to now having no art supply budget I put my cargo van to good use and visited several paint stores and asked for their oops paint. Oops paint is miss-tinted paint that people returned or was mixed incorrectly, so it is given away for free. I went to one paint store nearby in South Carolina. Upon entering the town I could immediately see that they had probably produced very few Rhodes Scholars. They had a room filled up to the ceiling with thousands of gallons of paint. Someone needed to go back to school and take Paint Mixing 101.

Hell with the school budget being nixed, I now had house paint and a wealth of creative ideas.

The following Monday morning I pulled my cargo van up closely to one of the back doors of the high school to unload the paint. When my second period class came around, which was my special needs class, I had them help me carry in all the paint. I thought this would be a good opportunity to instill trust in them as a group and as individuals. I appointed Johnny to be the supervisor. It would be his job to stand inside the cargo van and give orders to everyone else. With 200 gallons of paint to transport up two stories using an elevator, I thought this would be one of those break through moments where my trust as a teacher would give birth to hope and confidence, great self-esteem and leadership. (Romantic thinking can be costly).

Johnny was thrilled to be the boss. He was situated in the back of the van amidst an armory of paint cans like Black Beard standing proudly before his band of pirates. As he stood his ground, hands on his hips spouting off orders, a mutiny suddenly erupted. Ignoring Johnny, the rest of the class wanted a chance at standing in the truck looking cool. Soon everyone was in the back of the truck shouting out orders to each other. Johnny kept yelling "no, no, no, no!" One of Johnny's issues was that the word no was the only word he could pronounce correctly so he always worked it into every conversation—which created innumerable problems.

I felt sad for Johnny on so many levels. His mother was a crack addict and prostitute who abandoned him, as well as a brother and his older sister, at the door of a mental asylum. Upon getting her act together, she got her kids back and tried to raise them once again. One night, years later, his sister threw a birthday party for her baby's first birthday. Johnny's sister was divorced and her ex-husband showed up hours late to his own son's party. Shockingly, in sight of everyone there, he pulled out a gun, pointed it at his ex-wife's forehead and pulled the trigger. Johnny witnessed the whole nightmare. It is not difficult to see where Johnny's baggage came from.

Eventually, Johnny got control of the situation in the van full of paint cans. Slowly, one by one, each of the young men filed out of the van and began to pick up a gallon of paint in each hand. They shuffled along the trek to the second floor like they were climbing Mt. Everest in a blizzard. I walked along with them carrying my own gallons of paint, leaving Johnny alone in the van.

When I went back to the van after the third trip I heard Johnny yelling at Andre to get to work. Andre was the artist in the group. He was always dreaming out loud with his eyes wide open. This day he was simply walking around in circles and staring at the sky like he was having an epiphany of some sort. All the special needs students yelled at Andre to quit dreaming and come help them. Andre smiled politely at everyone and seemed glad to help. Johnny handed him a gallon of yellow paint to carry. When Andre picked it up he was overwhelmed by the weight of the gallon and dropped it by mistake on the sidewalk. Yellow paint splattered everywhere!

As the gallon of paint lay on its side emptying itself onto the sidewalk everyone just stood and stared in silence. I quickly ran, grabbed the paint and turned it upright. Yellow paint had spread out to a three-foot diameter ring. My students had it on their clothes and shoes and were now running around yelling "Ooooooohhhhhh nnnnnnooooooooooo, Mrrrrr. Bonnnnnneeellllllll!" Johnny started yelling at Andre, "No, no, no, no, no, no, no, no!" Another one of my boys kept yelling, "We-in-trouble-now-we-in-trouble-now-we-in-trouble-now!" The bell rang for classes to change and now students were flooding out the back doors facing a major roadblock. One of the boys named Reshin just stood there looking at the paint in shock. Reshin had great difficulty pronouncing any word in the English language correctly and he just pointed and stared at the paint yelling, "It-tilled, it-tilled, it-tilled, it-tilled."

An hour later everyone was as cleaned up as possible and settled into his or her next class. I was stuck with cleaning up the paint. I turned the van's ignition on and tried to pull off to park but the van hardly moved. I could smell the strong odor of burning rubber. What was going on? I looked down to discover more help from Johnny, the emergency break was on.

Chapter Seventeen

The Scream

To become accustomed to beauty, fix your eyes on the sublime.

—Jean Auguste Dominique Igres

THE NAME EDVARD MUNCH is synonymous with the painting *The Scream*[10]. It is one of the most recognizable images in the world presenting an agonized figure against a blood red sky. You can hear the shrieks coming from this haunting spirit of an image. Is this a ghost or a person? Either one, it is surely painful to look at too long.

I also know another spirit and once aware of his inner shrieks, he is also painful to look at for too long. This is Sharome, one of my special needs wheelchair students. Besides being severely mentally challenged, unable to talk, blind and having cerebral palsy, Sharome has no muscles in his neck to suspend his head upright. Therefore he appears to always be looking down at the ground as he sits strapped into his wheelchair looking like some harnessed-in drag racer that has lost a contact lens. Due to his frozen statuesque posture he is forced to drool on himself all day long. Because he cannot stand or walk his leg muscles remain in a state of atrophy so severely that you swear there is only bone and no muscle in the legs of his pants.

Sharome appeared to define the word broken. A living train wreck—a living scream.

This young man, this teenager, is like one of those beat up books that you find in a used bookstore. You look at the book and wonder why it was never tossed out. The binder is broken. The pages are dog-eared. Coffee stains dominate the cover. It is not until you make an effort to see beyond the cover and force yourself to pick the book up and read a page or two that you discover not everything is as it seems on the surface. The inverted nature of things must always be sought, even castles in the sky.

This broken book holds within insight unknown. A new definition of beauty you've never read about is revealed, not seen with the eye but with the spirit. Such is the existence beyond the cover inside of this young 19 year old used book sitting obscurely in a wheelchair, head down, no neck—that no one would ever open the cover to.

On the second day of class I knelt down and picked Sharome's head up from its usual neck-less downward attention and held it balanced on his shoulders. I got just an inch from his face. I said, "Gooooood mooooorning Sharome!" His eyes widened and he delivered an African smile that even Obama would be jealous of.

I soon discovered that Sharome loved music, especially the King of Pop, Michael Jackson. During the last fifteen minutes of each class I would go over to a computer and put on some MJ tunes and crank up the speakers as loud as they could go.

Sharome could not move his body in any manner so instead he would quiver or gyrate as if he were having a seizure. When he would first hear the music he would get so excited that he would attempt to throw his head back, and then he would open his mouth as wide as it could go, and then let out a large scream of joy. If you did not know he was happy you would think the scream was one of great distress.

The whole class would be dancing along with Sharome. I would take Sharome's wheelchair and move it with the music. Eventually I discovered moves with the chair that were safe for Sharome but offered the feeling of movement for him so he could feel the music. One motion I called The Astronaut. I would take Sharome's wheelchair and gently bring it back towards me until it almost touched the ground. He loved it every time.

It got to be that when I would enter the room each day to teach my special needs class Sharome could hear my voice and he would start moving in his wheelchair with excitement knowing that he would soon be dancing. It was as if he were woken out of a bad dream when I came in and soon the music would start, then sheer screams of joy would erupt.

One morning, during my commute, I found myself very depressed. An overwhelming feeling of emotional apathy hit me like an unsuspecting deer in the road. The thought that I was driving over an hour each day to instruct students in art seemed futile and a waste of time. Was there any real value in my giving to the students at all? Could I continue to do this ritual day after day when it counted for just a small paycheck?

That morning as I was taking Sharome's wheelchair and dancing, with him screaming in joy, my answer came quickly and unexpectedly. Even if my only reason to go through this personal trial were to give Sharome a life for a few minutes each day then that was more than sufficient for me. My commute, my selfish depression and my lousy paycheck became a small price to pay to give a few minutes of joy, even a life to Sharome. I had sunken into a selfishly made form of quicksand but Sharome pulled me out.

A few days later an administrator saw me moving to Michael Jackson with Sharome and his wheels. The play-it-safe-by-the-rules authority ended our dancing. There was never any risk with my dropping Sharome. I held him as safe as a new born but that was our last dance. Now when I enter the special needs class Sharome jerks out of joy to dance when he hears my presence but it is only a hope deferred. As the days passed, Sharome was moved out of my class, because it appeared that the staff could not tell the difference between his screams of joy or his screams of painful restriction from no longer dancing, from no longer living for a few minutes every day. Now whenever I see Edvard Munich's painting *The Scream*, I can only think of Sharome.

Ingres stated, "To become accustomed to beauty, fix your eyes on the sublime." It makes me wonder what Sharome thinks of as beauty, being blind, mentally challenged and strapped to a backbone called a wheelchair. Perhaps his world is all sublime?

Then again, perhaps there is no word or painting to begin to describe his world like *The Scream*.

Chapter Eighteen

The Fight

A work of art should be like a well-planned crime.
—Constantin Brancusi

THE FIRST WEEK OF the second semester was almost over. Spring was going to be arriving on the afternoon bus and I was going to greet her with a lustful kiss. I was imagining walking with Claude Monet,[11] the French Impressionist painter, and one of his sexy French models flashing some cleavage my way as I was strolling to my first class. Monet loved nature's spectrum of colors so much that he built a barn over a pond at his home in the south of France so he could paint year round, bringing to life the sensual colors of the water and its lilies. His art was not about ponds or landscapes or water lilies but it was all about seductive color to the eye. Monet died in 1926 but he was walking right beside me this morning describing to me how he was seduced by color in his later years in ways that were as powerful as his beautiful French model that walked beside him. My waking dream was shattered abruptly by a fight in the center of the school.

You can always tell when a fight has broken out. Students are running to the scene like someone is handing out $100 dollar bills. There is screaming and laughing. The students of Beach High love a good fight. As entertainment goes, nothing beats it— pardon the pun.

It was only 7:50am on a Thursday morning and two male students were beating the crap out of each other. This was no scuffle, this was a fist to face battle to draw blood and the color of red was everywhere. A female teacher began crowd control as dozens of students ran from distances to get a good ringside seat. The two guys going at it were huge. I jumped into the fight and grabbed one student from his back, trying to pull him off the other guy. When I grabbed him I realized he was three times my strength and that if he chose to he could simply turn around and deck me in seconds. Yet as I yelled over and over, "break it up!" he slowly gave into my pulling him off. It was as if he wanted the fight to end but only in honor, pretending that I had the muscle power to pull him back. He was bleeding badly. He had been punched in the mouth and was now spitting out blood.

I had always promised my wife that I would never break up a fight. Some students carry weapons and it would be easy for a teacher to become a statistic instead of a hero. One has to ask if it would be worth it. After all, that is why there are campus police. But that day I could not just stand there and do nothing. I defied my own logic for the gut feeling of doing the right thing. Still, maybe I should have just let them beat the crap out of each other.

Why had this kid I grabbed allowed me to end the fight under the illusion that I had actually broken it up by my own strength? This student was physically huge and strong, yet he was still just a boy in a man's body. As I held him from the back with his arms behind him he just stared at the ground with an apathetic gaze as if he were saying, "What the hell does life matter?" I understood that feeling myself. I was bordering on bankruptcy, I couldn't find a way to pay my every day bills, and often I had to beg for loans to survive another month. That week I had to borrow cash from another teacher to afford gas to get me back to the island. In one year my wife got cancer, I got laid off a job after 15 years of service and I was in a major car accident with my son. I felt like this student's affect was my self-portrait.

Suddenly with his head still bowed like a tent revival penitent and bleeding profusely from the mouth like a defeated boxer this boy giant was grabbed by a towering officer and escorted away. Now he was facing suspension from school placing him back on the streets. Now he could sharpen up on his fighting skills within a gang in order to do greater damage next time.

In a matter of seconds everything was back to Beach High normal—school bells buzzing, profanity ringing and students laughing at the two figures being herded away.

"Good morning and welcome to Beach High School," I murmured to myself as I walked, exhausted, to my first block class.

Monet left town with his French model.

Chapter Nineteen

Sally

There is spirit behind beauty—that is its cause.
—John F. Carlson

PABLO PICASSO[12] WAS AN expert at breaking things. He gave us a way to see a subject within a three dimensional realm as if we could walk around the subject without moving an inch. By breaking down a subject and reconstructing it in an unconventional manner we glean a greater depth of what we are seeing. A new form of beauty emerged from his brush via cubism.

Sally is in my special needs class. Sally is white in an all black class. Sally is in a wheel chair. Sally has beautiful brown hair. Sally can't talk. Sally has a spine that is contorted. Sally has a mind—that is perfect.

Picasso once said that everyone is an artist until the age of six. The simplicity of faith and expression is purest in a child. This is why we saw Picasso, Matisse and other great Masters of modern art seeking the creatively primitive and innocent vision in their work the last few years of their lives. To see the intended beauty of the brokenness of a line or bold stroke of color was to see correctly. Sally is such a line.

Sally's perfectly normal mind was placed inside a distorted broken shell of a body, strapped into a wheelchair and then placed within a class that is mentally challenged. She had to feel isolated, alone and mad as hell. At times, though she couldn't talk, she would simply start screaming. Was she in pain? Was she placed in her wheel chair incorrectly? I think she was simply mad at life and it was her only means of expression.

With pretty brown hair and eyes to match she could flash a gorgeous smile worth a fortune. She would have made the head of the cheerleading squad, homecoming queen or class president. In order to see her actual beauty you had to spend time really looking directly at her. The problem with Sally was that to look at her was to witness a painful existence, like watching a car wreck over and over.

One assignment I gave my special needs class was to create a self-portrait from a photograph. I would go from student to student and help each one create a beautiful portrait of themselves, taking their hands and guiding the pencil on the paper I attempted to create a magical portrait using their very own hands. Sally's hand was contorted and strapped down. She was unable to even lift her arm. I gently took her hand and carefully placed a pencil in it and started drawing her portrait as if she were drawing it. It was then, as I stared at her face for a long period of time, drawing her portrait, that I began seeing who she really was. Defining beauty, Thomas Aquinas said, "Beauty is that which pleases in mere contemplation." Problem is, in a society obsessed by time, contemplation is a rare word indeed.

It is human nature to not want to view human suffering. How many times do we skip over those long television appeals for world hunger while we finish off a quart of Haagen-Daz? When we do make a donation to world hunger, AIDS, or suffering children do we give just enough to ease the false guilt or do we choose to suffer for the need through giving sacrificially—out of pain? In the same manner, we often choose to ignore the pain directly in front of us. It is in our nature to run from pain, not run to it.

As a rich nation we design our highways far from the poor so we can't see them. We don't spend our tax dollars for education to help the needy but we build the roads to go around them. Education often ranks last in priorities.

We make ourselves blind out of selfishness, greed, and our ethnocentric ego that tells us that we have a right to the American Dream. I am guilty of being so foolishly blind and my credit score is exhibit A.

I finished Sally's portrait and held it up to her so she could see it. A smile landed on her face as if she had just been asked out to the prom. I hit a homerun for once as a teacher, and it felt good. But who really was the teacher?

Sally helped me to see through my foolish blindness of 50 years, to confront my superficial sight. Though Sally's spine was contorted, it was not she who was a skewed human being. Unknown to me, it was my sight that was contorted. John F. Carlson got it right: There is spirit behind beauty—that is its cause.

Chapter Twenty

Illusions

"A beautiful thing never gives so much pain as does failing to hear and see it."
—Michelanglo

SOMETIMES WHAT WE SEE doesn't really exist. Sometimes what does exist we don't really see. The main question becomes, what is real?

In the 60s and the 70s artists and philosophers posed this question more than any other time in history, expressed through a philosophy that builds on the famous French philosopher, Jean Baudrillard[13] and his concept of simulacra, a form of reality born out of a false reality. This act of appropriation[14] was to replace landscape with semiotics. From such a perception Pop Art was born, whereby we choose symbols to represent our existence as a culture. The problem with this path is that we get further and further into our semiotics as symbols of a life that by now has turned into an illusion of the past. Out of our illusions we create what we think is real, only it is actually hyper real, and a distorted Disneyland reality is birthed.

Daniel Bonnell

I have lived most of my life within a vacuum of illusions. Problem was, I never saw them. That's why they are called illusions, I suppose. Looking back, most of my life has been dominated by illusionary paths.

Illusions as simulacra come in all shapes and sizes. Here are a couple of examples: When we fall in love are we falling in love with the presentation of the person or the actual individual? The real presentation of the person you married makes its appearance only after the honeymoon. Our perception was an illusion. One of the greatest illusions of the 21st century happened on 9/11. Muslim terrorists were under the illusion that God wanted thousands of innocent people to die along with dozens of innocent men, women and children on three planes. Eventually this grand illusion led America into a war. Illusion or not, it is the simulacra that the militant Islamists follow.

This was not the first illusion that led Americans to war though. The Civil War era was the darkest period in American history. A form of simulacra (false reality) was established that condoned slavery. Beginning with the Civil War itself and its post Jim Crow era, the South bought into the simulacra that slavery was a right and a privilege. Its argument that slavery was approved in the Bible and that even the Father of our country, George Washington himself, owned 125 slaves—was proof enough for their argument.

The established illusion, now a concrete form of simulacra was reality based for those that chose to believe it. The Civil War ended the legal form of slavery but it did not end the spirit that established such a simulacra. The spirit of that false illusion landed as Jim Crow. It was perpetuated through the Ku Klux Klan and remained a strong illusion for another 90 years, leaving a wake of over 3,500 recorded lynchings.[15] My own family heritage stands guilty to this end when an innocent black man was falsely accused and lynched by the false accusation of a great cousin of mine for a murder my relative committed.

In order to bring a rational explanation to the difficult position I found myself in I resolved that it was by a divine directive. I chose to believe that the dove that visited me in the parking lot at my interview, and the fact that I was hired even without a teaching certificate, were not accidents but were God's purpose. I also realized that if I could survive a year or two of this new job that I would come out a better painter. My art was largely about human suffering and redemption, so what better teaching for me than observing within this demographic?

At age 50 I found myself chasing a rabbit down a hole. I had become Alice. Beach, however, was no wonderland, though just as strange. The nagging question about life for me was direct and painful; it is the truest of questions, what is true and what is simply an illusion?

Had I romanticized my teaching in the inner city or was I just not willing to admit my need for a job—any job? Should I have continued working the gallery scene or was I living in denial in being something that I am not? Am I a denier of self? Perhaps I was simply an embarrassment to myself and I had to lie to myself to cope with my reality? I had to live in the question long enough to discover the truth of the question—if I did not become an alcoholic first.

I chose to bring a form of appropriation into my classroom by creating fake legs hanging from the ceiling of my classroom, forcing the question of—what is true? The dangling legs appeared as if there were students sitting above the tile ceiling. I also created the illusion of a student sleeping on top of the art supply cabinet. At first glance it fools everyone. They are a daily reminder that we choose our illusions. They are a daily reminder that we need to re-evaluate our perceptions as we make the choices to adopt them as real. Our perceptions turn into presumptions when they go from being positive to pessimistic, such as when an I can perception turns into an I can't presumption.

The illusionary dangling legs and fake sleeping student served as a constant reminder for my students to be aware that they can only change their lives by challenging what they believe is true and real in their lives.

This reality was played out in a comical manner one day. The school had an annual drug search from classroom to classroom. The routine was that a Police Officer would enter the classroom, make a speech about the drug search and then lead all the students out into the hallway to be searched for weapons and drugs. A Police dog would search the empty room for drugs during the hallway shake down.

Not familiar with my illusionary students, the officer and his K9 entered the classroom once it was empty. In the hallway I heard the officer come on the radio to call for a back up as he exclaimed that students were trying to, "dodge the search by hiding in the ceiling!"

Chapter Twenty-One

Stormie

"What I've attempted to do, is establish a world through art in which the validity of my Negro experience could live and make its own logic."
—Romare Bearden

IN ORDER TO GET my students to learn to see beyond the use of their eyes I challenge them to see using their five senses and their mind's eye by creating a self-portrait of imagery made up of symbols, animals, places and things. It was to be a collage, which Romare Bearden[16] was a master of. I would ask, "If your life were a piece of music what would it sound like as you stare into the morning mirror before you brush your teeth. How would you visualize those sounds through imagery?" For one of my students named Stormie I feared that the music that defined her life had either not been written yet or was a collection of sounds that reflected her name.

She shared with me about her daily routine wherein she would awake off a roach infested couch, waking up her baby to a warm bottle of milk and leaving for an early school bus. Because there was no running water she had to go to the neighbor downstairs who always put a bottle of water outside the door each night for Stormie to retrieve. Her baby was left with the mother of her new boyfriend with whom she now temporarily lived with. Her boyfriend was serving prison time for armed robbery. Together the three of them lived in one of those hidden apartment houses on the corner of the dangerous intersection of an area only fit for selling used tires.

On a good morning her baby was fed and went back to sleep before 6:30am in time for her bus. On a bad morning she would have to let her baby cry away in his crib, waking her boyfriend's mother in annoyance and anger. Then Stormie had to face her wrath after school as if she were a fresh piece of steak being tossed to a starving lion.

Stormie's real mother was a drug addict. She had been born a crack baby with a deformed left hand and a brain condition that threatened her life.

Stormie once told me about a nightmare of an experience she went through. Her oldest sister, age 9, was being beaten to a pulp by her mother who was high on crack for no known reason. "I'll kill you right now you little fucking bitch!" she would scream over and over. She recalls the force of her mother's fist turned into a fleshly hammer as it pounded her face with each blow being harder than the one before it. The scene turned as she recalled blood pouring out of her sister's mouth and nose as she crawled across the cold linoleum floor trying to escape. The screams of her being beaten to near death brought the police to the door. Stormie was afraid of the police. This fear was born out of years of her Mother's drug busts, watching her being hauled off to jail and Stormie and her sister being left with an angry, verbally abusive neighbor. As Stormie opened the door for the police, she ran out. She found herself running down the middle of a dark street into the night.

As I finished taking roll during my second block class the front office called me over the intercom to send Stormie to the front office to leave. In shock Stormie gathered her books and slung her backpack over her shoulder, glanced at me out of a hidden embarrassment and walked out the door.

As she walked into the front office she was handcuffed and arrested. The charge was for being a runaway youth. She was booked, fingerprinted and placed in the county jail for two weeks until a preliminary trial could take place. At the hearing Stormie explained that her mother had thrown her out of the house and she had no place to go except her boyfriend's mother's house. The judge asked the mother if this was true at which point her mother went off into a tirade of profanity and mental insanity. The judge threw the case out and Stormie was free to go.

Stormie came back to school and told me her story. I sat in my class alone after all my students had filed out at the end of the day, thinking about the black painter Romare Bearden's quote, "What I've attempted to do, is establish a world through art in which the validity of my Negro experience could live and make its own logic." Certainly Stormie's life was a valid experience in spite of her circumstances, but what happened to her was completely unreasonable. Logic disappeared like this runaway teen in her collage self-portrait.

Chapter Twenty-Two

Look Around

Recommend virtue to your children. That alone, not wealth, can give happiness. I speak from experience. It upholds me in adversity and the thought of it and my art prevent me from putting an end to my life.

—Ludwig van Beethoven

THERE IS AN HOUR when night seems to be close to death—when mind, body and soul are alive only by a shallow breath. The blow from the ax fell within such an hour.

Robert Bonnell (my distant cousin) was rabid mad because of some money that was owed him and in a senseless moment he killed his uncle. The next day he blamed the murder on a slave and there was a lynching before sundown. Southern roots can be risky to unveil.

I fled my southern roots for many years. I was the first one in my family to not go to the University of Georgia, but art school. Let there be no doubt, my DNA has kudzu on it and a side of biscuits and gravy. I was born a southerner. Two of my relatives died in the Civil War as Confederates. My own grandmother did not know that white people worked until she was age thirteen. With a heritage like that

I guess I can't get any more southern in my bones and no, I do not keep an axe in my house, my wife won't let me.

Jump ahead 145 years after the Civil War. Look around my classroom. There is not a child here that has a father. Look around my classroom. The students wear memorial t-shirts of friends and family members that were killed over the summer due to gang wars, domestic violence, and drugs. Look around my classroom. You see students that are sleeping because they work into the morning at some lousy job to help bring home some groceries for their mom. Look around my classroom. Almost half of my class will go into the military because they can't afford to get into college. Look around my classroom. Only half the students are given a free lunch, the other half starves because their parents can't afford to give them lunch money. Look around my classroom. Over half the students are dealing drugs to help pay the bills at home. Look around my classroom. I have high school seniors that have only been to downtown Savannah once in their whole life because of fear of what exists beyond Martin Luther King Drive. Look around my classroom. At least two of my female students have a child at home or are expecting. Look around my classroom. Within each of my classes at least three of my female students have been raped, even as children. Look around my classroom. At least four of my students within each class have never seen their real fathers because they are in prison. Look around my classroom. Not one student can tell me who the Pope is, what the word Catholic, Protestant or Anglican means, how many branches of Government there are, or can say the National Anthem all the way through.

There is no doubt that prejudice and social slavery still exists in America and will for a long time, even after electing a black president. If Dr. Martin Luther King Jr. were sitting in my class he would want to go back to sleep and keep on dreaming.

Chapter Twenty-Three

Soul Food

Sex and beauty are inseparable. Beauty is experience, nothing else; it is not an arrangement of features; straight nose, large eyes, etc. It is something felt, a glow or a communicated sense of fineness. Even the plainest person can look beautiful, can be beautiful.
—D.H. Lawrence

I BLAME IT ON a black church that I attend on occasion—getting me turned onto soul food. I put on weight just thinking about it. After Sunday services a free lunch is served up. I sat down to what I thought was a plate of barbecue chicken that was fantastic. Pretty soon I started spitting out bones that were plentiful. I discovered the bones were knuckles and I had been eating pig's feet. The following Sunday I had ox tail and it was delicious. Slaves were great cooks. They could take any scrap that the plantation owner would throw out and turn it into a savoring gourmet meal. Pig's feet, oxtail, cow intestines and more all became the main courses at the slaves' table. The same great cuisine remains years later.

There's no question about it, the best food in the world is found in the Lowcountry. There's no question about it, the worst food in the world is found in the Lowcountry.

Obesity is nothing new in America. It exists even within poor demographics. I often wonder how 80% of my students are at the poverty level yet remain obese? The bottom line is that these kids only have a single mom at home and she cooks with butter and fatback without a second thought. Butter and fatback is to the Lowcountry what garlic and olive oil are to Italy.

Soul food may be good for the soul but it's hard on the waistline.

Homecoming was approaching Beach. Nominations for Homecoming Queen were coming in and soon the Homecoming court would be parading itself around at pep rallies. The shocker was that all the nominations were obese young ladies. In the Homecoming Pep rally they would walk up and down the court like supermodels, strutting their stuff as they gave a proud wave to the crowd as if each of them were blue-blooded royalty.

I then realized that these young ladies had incredible self-esteem. They did not suffer with the average, normal teenage girl, Britney Spears body image that made them all a bit freakish. In fact these young black teens were happier than any of those wanna-be-phony-queens. Perhaps the "soul" in the food has essential ingredients that also feed the spirit?

Pass the grits and gravy please.

Chapter Twenty-Four

Being Thankful

"When we are no longer children, we are already dead."
—Brancusi

I AM BLIND AND foolish. As a student within a post slavery culture one of my biggest lessons I am seeking to learn is one of the simplest—the importance of being thankful. It is a lesson that a child could learn quickly. Problem is I am too much of an adult, blind and foolish.

One Sunday morning while sitting in church, a black church, I witnessed this simple virtue being played out over and over. The Deacon of the church was praying out loud before the whole congregation saying, "Lord, thank you for a good nights sleep! Lord, thank you that we could wake up and come here this morning! Lord, thank you for the air that we breathe! Lord, thank you for the clothes we have on our backs! Lord, thank you for the roofs that are over our heads! Lord, thank you, thank you, thank you!"

I sat there judging the prayer. How simplistic. Let's pray about the things that matter, the war in Iraq, the economy, the crime rate. It seemed like a good waste of time when it comes to prayer. Before I finished my next breath

I realized how pious, judgmental, and self-righteous I was. Ashamed, I turned my hands upside down on my lap, opened the palms of my hands, and outwardly received the lesson of being thankful.

Driving home from church that day I realized that such a teaching came from a heritage of slavery. Day by day a slave only had his mind, body and spirit, not a home, money and a future. They learned to live in the moment, to be present, to breathe, sleep, eat and love.

The following week I witnessed this lesson being born out through various black teachers. One particular woman named Ms. Firs was such a thankful soul. Whenever I would ask her how she was that day she always proclaimed, "I'm blessed!" Yet I knew that she and her husband were going through one trial after another, from financial problems to struggles with their two sons. Her husband was a truck driver who owned his own truck yet it was always in the shop. At the end of each month there was only enough money from his hauling to make a payment on the truck. One son was in jail for drug possession and the other one was in jail for driving without a license and stealing a car. Still, she remained positive every day, prayed and wept for her sons everyday and always stayed thankful.

One morning, when Ms. Firs asked me how I was I let the bottom fall out of my response like an unexpected down poor. I dumped on her all my problems. Lack of sleep, living hand to mouth and trying to survive on a teacher's low salary had gotten the best of me.

Later that same day after the last school bell rang and students began their way home the classroom sat in shadows with light bursting through the windows at a forty-five degree angle. A gentle knock came at my door. Ms. Firs entered. "Mr. Bonnell I'm gonna anoint you with holy water that my pastor blessed and I want to pray over you," she said. For a spit second I was shocked. Then humbled. Then broken. Then grateful.

I quickly realized that she is not just an individual that one dumps their problems on. She does something about your problems, even if praying over you is the only visible means of extending help. So I saw an opportunity to humble myself and let her pray away as she poured water over my head. It was quite a wonderful and strange moment. This woman who had far more struggles and pain in life than I could count was out to help relieve me of my struggles and pain. Did her prayers and holy water help me the next day or weeks to come? Probably, I just don't remember but one thing did change for me.

Now when people ask me how I'm doing, I take a deep breath, think for a moment and respond, 'I'm blessed.'

Chapter Twenty-Five

The Divine Proportion

Painting is the grandchild of nature. It is related to God.
—Rembrandt

When I stood in front of her I was blown away. I was standing in front of the most beautiful woman in the world. Who would have dreamed it? It was the fantasy of every artist to behold her in all her beauty and mystery—a super model from Madison Avenue?

No, the Mona Lisa.

It is no mystery that Leonardo da Vinci[17] and Michelangelo[18] used a creative mathematical model called the divine proportion[19], also known as the golden mean and Phi. It was a math equation with the ratio of 1.618 that produces a spiral type graph, which breaks the area space up into proportions leaving a beautiful form of composition that artists could apply to their work.

I think back to when I stood in front of my first class of students at Beach. I was blown away standing in front of students that had never heard of a single artist or museum in the world. They could not name one piece of created art in history. They had no concept of beauty on such a level.

85

Another manner of understanding this ratio or curve is to ask why a violin or any string instrument is tuned to a certain pitch and tone? There exists a vibration or ratio of beauty that is also aesthetic to sound.

The divine proportion took on the name Phi after the Greek sculptor Phidias who first studied the ratio our brains tune to when we consider beauty. Thus the sensual curves that evoke our sexual desires are viewed within every few inches on the female anatomy, the divine proportion becomes sensual proportions. The brain mysteriously is tuned to acknowledge beauty when this ratio lines up with our brains through sight, like a radio dial tunes into a station.

Spiral jetties are a classic form of the divine proportion. If you observe a river you discover that its margins are built on spiral jetties; those curving whirlpools of water that are detoured by rocks, and trees. A whole other life exists within those river jetties of fish and moss and rock formations. It is often in the spiral jetties of our everyday life that we actually live out our lives and discover that which is most valuable to us. This is probably because it is within our removing ourselves from the main current of life that we take the time to see the best.

The Hubble telescope reveals images of our universe and galaxy that are formed using the divine proportion. It is all one beautiful curve that turns into itself as a form of a gracious, colorful, whirlpool. All of nature it seems contains the divine proportion. It's hard to find a flower that does not contain it, or a leaf or a seashell. Even a dolphin holds the beauty of the ratio in its curvatures.

What happens if our brains are tuned to the wrong scale? What kind of a tuning fork is required for someone who has never been tuned correctly before? I have only one student with a father living at home. All the rest of my students are living with their single mother, mostly as "latch key" kids. The norm is to always be striving to make ends meet, keep your sons or daughters out of a gang or from selling drugs or getting pregnant.

The social slavery that exists in the Lowcountry is unlike anywhere else in the country that I have experienced. Perhaps its roots are deep within the hopelessness of social advancement as it was in the days of slavery 150 years ago? There are over 600 families in and around Beach High School. The average income is $18,000 per year. That's $4,000 below the national poverty level.

I thought that such beauty, of such a ratio, was hard pressed to find in a place like Beach, but I am wrong. Actual beauty exists everywhere, but we fail to see it. This is the purpose of this book. Suffering brings to light the essence of life, which is always about redefining love. Whether it be forgiving others, loving your enemies or dancing with someone in a wheelchair.

Perhaps there exists a hidden aesthetic of beauty within such a culture—within such a dark past that meets the divine ratio and even exceeds it? Perhaps it is a ratio that Leonardo da Vinci even saw and this might be the real mystery behind the smile of the Mona Lisa.

Chapter Twenty-Six

Dan the Pastry Man

Art is an intersection of many human needs.
—Carl Andre

"Mr. Bonnell, do you have anything to eat?" came a question from one of my students named Kahlid. It was 12:00 noon and I was standing in the hall welcoming my students into class. "What would you want to eat, Kahlid, if I did have food?" I asked. "A cinnamon bun because it's filling, I'm hungry as hell," he replied as he quickly ran to his next class. The next morning I stopped on my way to work at a gas station and bought him the biggest cinnamon bun I could find. Kahlid was shocked that I thought of him that day as I watched him devour the pastry in seconds.

After taking a poll in my classroom, I discovered that most of my students did not eat breakfast because their single parent lifestyle could not afford it. In fact, if not for receiving lunch at school many of them did not eat at all.

On my way home from school that day I stopped at a dozen supermarkets and bakeries asking them about their day old pastry and if they could donate them to my class. No one would donate to the cause. A local food bank had beat me to it.

Before I went home that day I stopped at the local Starbucks to inquire about their pastries as well. I came to find out that the local food bank had continually failed to pick up the pastry on a regular basis. The manager, sensing my desire to obtain the pastry, promised me half the pastry instead. Upon coming back the next day she gave me all she had on the shelf. My commitment to coming each day paid off and soon she dropped the food bank all together. She spread the word to other Starbucks in the area and soon I was picking up from three Starbucks each morning. There was enough to feed all three of my classes with breakfast or a snack each day, which added up to 60 students every day.

Soon, starving teachers and janitors started coming in my classroom begging for any breakfast pastry I had available. I kept a separate stash in a back room just for them. I had to hide the pastry between classes because of all the students who were not my students that would pour into my room in droves to see if they could grab some breakfast as well. Eventually, I quit hiding it and allowed anyone who was hungry to help themselves.

Now one may very well argue that a pastry from Starbucks is way too many calories, and that I should not have been feeding students such an unhealthy breakfast. Try selling that statement to a starving student on an empty stomach. I learned that there are many resources at our fingertips in the world, resources that are ours if we but look for them to meet a need for someone else other than ourselves. Over 200 students a week receive a free breakfast now. They all know where they can come to if they find themselves hungry. Kahlid still comes up to me for food now and then. He laughs out of unbelief as he sorts through dozens of Starbucks pastry until he finds a huge cinnamon bun.

Chapter Twenty-Seven

Being Present

Speed is the enemy of observation.
—Jacques-Yves Cousteau

OFTEN WE AMERICANS DON'T live in the moment. Instead we live in the moment to come. Problem is, if you are always living for a future moment, i.e. retirement, the pay raise that will change your life, or that day you will win the lottery—then you never actually live at all. Sadly, I think I have lived most of my life this way. I started having panic attacks at age 40 after I was fired from a New York Art Directors job. I started grinding my teeth and tried anti-depressants only to discover they made me more depressed. My hidden frustration of wanting to be a painter full time would float to the surface and I faced the monster of regret as if we were roommates in a lone jail cell.

I was never mindfully present to step outside of my life and see what I was doing to myself. I was like the patron that waited in line at the Louvre[20] for hours to get in and then walked quickly past the art, never really absorbing the beauty of the pieces. The need to see it all in a day made my spirit bankrupt but my mind happy.

Daniel Bonnell

To view great art you must be present before the work. You must let it speak to you and you must learn to listen. Your mind must retreat and your spirit must advance. It is only after you hear Beethoven's 5th and are raptured in the arrangements that you allow your mind to come out of the back seat to try to explain what the music was all about. Recently I visited the retrospective of William de Kooning's art at the Museum of Modern Art[21] (MOMA) in New York City. I overheard a guide explain his work on a surface level.

She described little areas of each painting that had certain fluid movements and she would reveal small details about the technique used by de Kooning to create an abstract painting level upon level. All her information was shallow and meaningless. It was all mind banter. One has to stand before a painting and wait, wait for it to talk. One must be present with humble ears to hear. You must be present before the art.

As a teacher to under privileged black students I found myself always trying to improve my lesson plans and come up with projects that educated and informed students in a more meaningful manner. I was missing the most important dynamic of being a teacher, an artist, and an adult. I was not present.

To be present requires being still and sitting. To be present requires listening. To be present is the easiest thing in the world to do. To be present is the hardest thing in the world to do.

I started simply sitting with my students and being present with them. At first most of them found it very uncomfortable. I became privy to their conversations that one would deem inappropriate for a teacher's ears. I made myself be with them all, sometimes doing the same projects that I had taught and sometimes just sitting and listening to the conversations.

I think there is an important form of intimacy with simply being with another human being saying nothing, doing nothing but just being. I think it is a statement to the other person that they are valuable to be around and that they are accepted.

One day I realized that perhaps my lack of being with others just for the sake of being could mean that I never really lived. My art is mostly about man being in his fallen human condition. The paintings are largely about death on a cross or being held. Life and death. Expulsion and embracing. Suffering and suckling. Sinner and innocence.

At the age of 18 months I was diagnosed with a form of illness that meant I had to be quarantined for a week. This meant that I was not allowed to see my parents except for a few hours each day and never at night. The doctors felt I would die and that I needed to be placed in an all white sterile room by myself to play out my illness.

Though I could not be held or comforted at night I went through a form of transformation that I cannot explain or fully remember. I do know that I was held. God was present.

Perhaps this is why my work is largely about the cross and being held; certainly it is about being present. While sitting with my students, just being, I still often feel that time is money and my life is far too important to just sit there, shut up and be still.

Chapter Twenty-Eight

Herbie

There is no excellent Beauty that hath not some strangeness in the proportions.
—Francis Bacon

I LIVED IN AFRICA years ago. I caught malaria. Malaria sucks. But this was just a small sample of the trials of survival that are an every day reality to Africans. Before Africa, I lived in a rescue mission in New York City. As a full time volunteer I caught scabies from the homeless in the process of helping them discard their old street clothes for newer ones. I felt their humiliation, especially when I went to a public clinic for the poor to discover what I had caught and how I caught it. When teaching at Beach I caught the suffering of not wanting to be in a place of unending longing to be somewhere else, or even worse—to be someone else. 'Beauty and the Beast' rises to the conscious surface. The opposite of all that I have experienced within these three settings was beauty itself. I had been living with the beast of suffering. It seemed, like my early dating life—Beauty always stood me up.

What is beauty? Is it in me? Do I see it? Where does it live? Can I get her phone number?

It is a sad reality that suffering always teaches life's most profound lessons. The lesson of love being birthed out of suffering is one that repeats itself over and over if we have eyes to see. My special needs students taught me this essential lesson from my first day at Beach High School but I was too blind to see it. The essential question they asked themselves silently about me on the first day of class years ago was do you love me?

This classroom of innocence did not care about titles or degrees. They did not care about appearance or status. They only wanted to be loved. Sure it sounds schmaltzy. Sure it sounds Pollyanna. Sure it sounds corny. But that question, if we are honest, is one that we ask of ourselves and of others every day. When you discover the need to be loved, then you learn that you can only obtain such love by presenting it to others. Even when your well is dry. Even when it costs.

Herbie was white in an all black special needs class that first year. He was chunky and could never look at you in the eyes. He would, at times, stand up in my class and aimlessly start dancing. His teachers would yell at him to sit down; he was always in trouble. I didn't care. Herbie had a buzz cut that made him look like a cartoon you would see in the Sunday comics 50 years ago. He couldn't do much but he could hug the breath right out of you. Herbie would insist on giving me a hug every day or he would not leave the room after class.

One day, at the end of my class, as my special needs students were filing out the door. Herbie found himself in great turmoil. I was on the other side of the class and everyone had left except him. He knew that his teachers would yell at him if he lingered behind. Standing there at the door, not knowing if he should risk crossing the room to hug me and get into trouble with his teachers or to run out the door to catch up with his class, Herbie was visibly upset. Suddenly he ran towards me, all the way across the room, gave me a hug like it was his last one and then ran back to catch his class who was long gone. As I poked my head out of the class I could hear Herbie being yelled at by the two paraprofessional teachers down the hall.

Herbie, by the world's standards, was a hopeless case. Unattractive, overweight, bad haircut and no rhythm—that's Herbie. However, Herbie knew how to love greatly; even when it cost him, even when there was a price to pay.

Herbie convicts me. I fail to love as completely as he does. Herbie's parents moved a month later to another state. I never saw him again. Damn.

My special needs kids accept me every day, when I'm up and when I'm down. When I am stressed out and ready to jump in front of a bus I will walk into their classroom and just sit with them, while being fully accepted, while being fully loved just as I am. Now when teaching at Beach I am no longer caught in the suffering of not wanting to be in a place of unending longing to be somewhere else. Beauty is . . . "strangeness in the proportions." Francis Bacon nailed it.

Afterword

A painter spends his life in despair trying to paint the beauty he sees and in so doing he approaches more beauty.
—Charles Hawthorn

I WOULD BE DISHONEST to any reader of this book if I were not transparent about my pursuit of Christology in becoming the art that I produce. The great medieval artist/teacher Fra Angelico,[22] an Italian Monk once stated, "To paint Christ one must live Christ." In the same manner my son and I heard the renowned cellist YoYo Ma. It was 9/11 and America was in a state of shock. YoYo Ma was to perform that night in Colorado Springs. The concert went on in spite of the tragedy of the day. My son and I had center aisle seats only five rows deep. YoYo Ma came out and changed his performance pieces. He would open his concert with a mass remembering the massive amount of lives lost on that dark day in America's history. With no music to read from he closed his eyes and embraced the cello as if he had to hold onto it to keep from exploding off the stage. No one existed in the great concert hall but he and his cello. He actually became one with the music, with his art. I left the concert hall a changed man that night. YoYo Ma had become one of my teachers.

I live and work with people that are cast to the bottom of society, fully realizing that I am actually no different than they are. To serve them with my art is an honor because through getting to know them, they too have become my teachers.

Most of my art is about the human condition of suffering within a realm of redemption. Great art always teaches us something we've never seen before. It is within this inverted form of reality that I find the real or the true. Alchemy is the pursuit of turning metal into gold. My desire is to find the gold within the metal, to tell stories that would never get told. "To see the David in the stone and release it," as Michelangelo once stated.

Each of my students is wrapped up in such a stone of imperfection and despairing beauty. I find the weight of my own stone less binding through seeking the release of others.

Endnotes

All Quotations from:
Donna Ward La Cour, Artists in Quoation. McFarland & Company, Inc. Publishers.

1. *Black Americans in Congress—The Negroes' Temporary Farewell*. Online: http://baic.house.gov/historical-essays/essay.html?intID=5&intSectionID=24
2. *Alfred Ely Beach Built the First New York Subway System*. About.com Inventors. Online: http://inventors.about.com/library/inventors/blbeach.htm
3. *The Persistence of Memory*, Museum of Modern Art, NYC. Online: http://www.moma.org/collection/object.php?object_id=79018.
4. Jonathan Fineberg, *Art Since 1940: Strategies of Being*, Third Edition, Prentice Hall, 165,166.
5. Les Demoiselles d'Avignon, *Pablo Picasso* (Spanish, 1881–1973), Museum of Modern Art, NYC. Online: http://www.moma.org/collection/object.php?object_id=79766
6. Rene Magritte, *A World History of Art*. Online: http://www.all-art.org/art_20th_century/magritte1.html.
7. The Laundress, *Honore' Daumier* (French Marseilles 1808-1879 Valmondois) The Metropolitan Museum of Art, NYC. Online: http://www.metmuseum.org/Collections/search-the-collections/110000529.
8. Jonathan Fineberg, *Art Since 1940: Strategies of Being*, Third Edition, Prentice Hall, 397.
9. Martin Stokstad, *Art History*, Second Edition, Prentice Hall, 984.
10. Ibid., 1038.
11. Ibid., 1018.
12. Ibid., 1072.
13. Jonathan Fineberg, *Art Since 1940: Strategies of Being*, Third Edition, Prentice Hall, 343.

14. Martin Stokstad, *Art History*, Second Edition, Prentice Hall, 1162.
15. New World Encyclopedia. Oneline: http://www.newworldencyclopedia.org/entry/Lynching
16. Jonathan Fineberg, *Art Since 1940: Strategies of Being*, Third Edition, Prentice Hall, 365–369.
17. Martin Stokstad, *Art History*, Second Edition, Prentice Hall, 88–690.
18. Ibid., 694–701.
19. H.E. Huntley, *The Divine Proportion*. Dover Publishers, 186.
20. The Louvre Museum. Oneline: http://www.louvre.fr/en.
21. The Museum of Modern Art (MOMA). Oneline: http://www.moma.org.
22. Martin Stokstad, *Art History*, Second Edition, Prentice Hall, 622.